GREAT PHILOSOPHERS

GREAT PHILOSOPHERS
A BRIEF STORY OF THE SELF AND ITS WORLDS

JEFFREY REID

broadview press

LIBRARY AND ARCHIVES CANADA CATALOGUING IN PUBLICATION

Reid, Jeffrey
    Great philosophers : a brief story of the self and its worlds / Jeffrey Reid.

ISBN 978-1-55111-963-2

    1. Philosophy—History. I. Title.

B72.R44 2009   190   C2008-907368-1

BROADVIEW PRESS is an independent, international publishing house, incorporated in 1985. Broadview believes in shared ownership, both with its employees and with the general public; since the year 2000 Broadview shares have traded publicly on the Toronto Venture Exchange under the symbol BDP.

We welcome comments and suggestions regarding any aspect of our publications—please feel free to contact us at the addresses above or at broadview@broadviewpress.com / www.broadviewpress.com.

NORTH AMERICA
Post Office Box 1243,
Peterborough, Ontario,
Canada K9J 7H5

2215 Kenmore Ave.,
Buffalo, New York, USA 14207
TEL: (705) 743-8990
FAX: (705) 743-8353

customerservice@broadviewpress.com

UK, IRELAND, & CONTINENTAL EUROPE
NBN International, Estover Road, Plymouth,
UK PL6 7PY
TEL: 44 (0) 1752 202300
FAX: 44 (0) 1752 202330
enquiries@nbninternational.com

AUSTRALIA & NEW ZEALAND
UNIREPS University of New South Wales
Sydney, NSW 2052 Australia
TEL: 61 2 96640999
FAX: 61 2 96645420
infopress@unsw.edu.au

Broadview Press acknowledges the financial support of the Government of Canada through the Book Publishing Industry Development Program (BPIDP) for our publishing activities.

Consulting Editor for Philosophy: John Burbidge
Designed and typeset by Em Dash Design

 This book is printed on paper
containing 100% post-consumer fibre.

Printed in Canada

To my loved ones

CONTENTS

INTRODUCTION

This book attempts to tell a story through the life of its protagonists. In terms of story-telling, there should be nothing surprising about this. It is generally the way narratives are constructed. The difference here, however, is that the lives of the main characters take place primarily in their ideas, and taken together, these ideas form a shared narrative called the Western philosophical tradition.

This narrative has been recounted many times before, in many different manners, and the names of at least some of the protagonists may be known to many people today, the same way literate citizens of Classical Athens were aware of the players and stories of the ancient Homeric tales. However, a shared, common story only stays alive if it is retold, recounted, reinterpreted and passed on. Most importantly perhaps, to stay alive a shared story must belong to those who share it. They must view the story with a sense of owner-ship, and yet be willing and even eager to partake in it with others, exactly as the indigenous Haida people of the Canadian west coast felt they could reveal their myths and legends to European ethnographers because the Haida knew the stories were theirs to share.

This book is my attempt to retell the story of the Great Philosophers. I do so because many people today may not know that the story actually belongs to them, that it is a great part of who they are. Only by remembering it and recognizing it as theirs will they ever be able to recount it to others. And it is a story worth telling.

My aim is to emphasize the strong narrative aspect of the Great Philosophers' tale, showing how each thinker's ideas form part of an on-going story line: trials are endured; obstacles are met and sometimes overcome, sometimes avoided; new paths are discovered; unexpected characters are introduced ... Like any great story, the end is reached when we can look back and recognize the narrative that we have been following as our own.

My goal is also to tell this story in an inviting, introductory way, to keep it short and readable. Some might object to such brevity and find cavalier and unfaithful the attempt to summarize the infinitely complex thought of each philosopher in so few pages. Indeed, it may be particularly galling to university philosophers, like me, to have "their" thinker dealt with in such summary fashion or to have the object of their life's research only mentioned in passing, or not at all. To readers looking for a more encyclopedic approach, I can do no more service than to refer them to such unsurpassed histories of philosophy as those by Frederick Copleston or Emile Bréhier.

Finally, in defense of brevity, I would say that the story of Western philosophy is ultimately a short one. It began only about 2,500 years ago, barely a heartbeat in the several million year development of the human race, nothing at all when set against the 13.7 billion years or so since time and the universe began. Yet through the brief window of Western philosophy, this pinhole of light, we have tried to see everything. In the history of humanity, and perhaps in the history of the universe, it would be hard to find a more audacious enterprise.

GREAT PHILOSOPHERS: WHO ARE THEY?

There is some agreement on who these philosophers are. Certain names impose themselves. Ask any group of Western philosophy professors to make a list of ten great philosophers and the chances are five names will show up on every list. The notion of greatness may be somewhat relative, but the fact that any group of academics can easily agree on at least five philosophers who are "great" means that there is a core of thinkers in the tradition who are inescapable. Why are they "great"? Why do we agree on the same names? What does it mean to be a "great" philosopher?

In order to answer such questions, we first must understand what it means to be a philosopher. There are many possible answers to this question. Originally it meant a lover of wisdom; in the popular imagination, a philosopher has come to be a solitary contemplator of things detached from any worldly importance, a quasi-religious or spiritual figure. I want to propose, for introductory purposes, a more realistic, down-to-earth definition.

First of all, being a philosopher means being part of a certain field of study. The same way a mathematician must participate in the field of mathematics, a philosopher must participate in the field of philosophy. What is a field of study? I would answer that it implies a specific set of objects. Mathematics, as a field of study, studies mathematical objects, numbers, operations, sets, equations, etc. Anthropology studies human cultural objects. Physics studies physical, natural objects. Philosophy, to be a field of study, therefore must study philosophical objects.

The idea of a field of study also implies a history of study. It means that there is a progression, that there is a story that makes sense. Somehow, things are linked together in a certain order that can be explained or recounted, understood and passed on. For example, if we're talking about mathematics as a field of study, we accept that each new mathematician builds on the history of mathematics as established by her predecessors. Similarly, in the field of geography, each new geographer builds on discoveries from the past.

This "building on" can mean several things: besides accepting and using the discoveries of the past, it can mean questioning and even overturning established knowledge. Nonetheless, the fact that a field of study has a history means that the prior efforts of those in the field must be taken into account; they cannot be simply forgotten. So, if philosophy is to be a field of study, it must have a history where the prior efforts of those in the field are taken into account, and must involve the study of specific objects. Philosophers are those who have participated in this field.

What are the objects specific to philosophy, which allow us to group together those who have studied them? Just as we can say there is something common in mathematical objects and that Euclid was a mathematician in 300 BCE, Ptolemy was a mathematician in 100 CE, Leibniz was a mathematician in 1700 and Poincaré was a mathematician in 1900, there must be something common in philosophical objects that allows us to say that Plato was a philosopher, Descartes was a philosopher, Hegel was a philosopher, Sartre was a philosopher ... What are these philosophical objects?

Let us concentrate, for now, on three: the self (a.k.a. the soul), the world (a.k.a. the universe) and God (a.k.a. the Good, the Absolute, Mother Nature ...). One might object that other fields share these objects, that they are not specific to philosophy. Indeed, psychology, for example, examines the self. Astronomy examines the cosmos. Physics deals with the world. Theology deals with God. However, before these individual sciences were created or acknowledged as specific fields, they were part of philosophy. In fact, the terms "philosophy" and "science" were virtually synonymous until well into the 19th Century. This means philosophy has a scientific aspect: the rigor of thought, of thinking and presenting thought in a reasoned discourse the Greeks called *logos*. Philosophy uses recognized forms of reasoning that seek to convince through their structural strength or validity. However, philosophy also has a poetic, metaphoric even mythical aspect, a speculative, contemplative side that is foreign to the way modern experimental science is generally seen today.

Whether or not philosophy is scientific, there is no doubt that, over its history, it has spun off the individual, specific sciences currently studied and pursued in universities and other centers of research. One might therefore wonder what is left of philosophy, having divested itself of the objects taken up by other fields of inquiry. If there is anything left at all, it is because there are certain questions or problems pertaining to the self, the world and God that remain beyond the scope of the other sciences. These questions or problems are the true objects of philosophy.

Regarding the world, geography can map it and tell us about its formations and configurations. Physics can investigate the quanta of matter and energy that make up the known world. Astronomy can fix the approximate age of the universe and establish the position and movement of galaxies and black holes. But only philosophy asks the question, "Why is there something rather than nothing?" Or, "What is the nature of being?" Or, "How do we know the world exists?" "How much of it can we know?"

Regarding the human world, economists can derive laws that explain the macro and micro-economics of human communities. Sociologists can describe social trends and movements, but philosophy asks, "What is human freedom and how is it possible?" Or, "What does it mean to be morally good?"

Regarding the self or the soul, psychologists may develop theories of human behavior or of mental pathology and treatment; neurologists plot the activity of the human brain, but philosophy asks, "What does it mean to be conscious?" Or, "Who am I?" Or, "How can I know others are conscious beings like me?" Or, "Where does this feeling of personal identity come from and does it really cease to exist when I die?" "What is the relation between my sense of self and my body?"

Regarding God, theologians may explain the Bible, or the Koran or the Torah. They may help answer questions of faith and interpret the doctrines of our religions, but philosophy asks, "How can I know God exists?" Or, "Can morality have meaning without God?" Or, "If God is perfect, why would he create something as imperfect as the world?" "Why do we refer to God in the masculine?"

Such an avalanche of "Big Questions" may seem both dizzying and childish. These are the sort of questions children ask, repeatedly, and then, as they reach maturity, drop as being naïve or immature. Indeed, there is always something childish about philosophical questioning, and mature, serious adults tend to find the overly inquisitive child both laughable and frustrating. Philosophers have often encountered this frustration from "no-nonsense" people, anchored in what is generally called the real world: "Why don't you just stop asking these futile questions and get on with it? Things are just as they are. What do you plan to do with that degree? Stop bothering me!"

To the extent that some of us live fairly comfortably in the world, we tend to share this "mature" attitude. It helps us pay the bills, do the shopping, get married, raise children. However, the chances are that at some time, perhaps in a long forgotten childhood moment, perhaps in a more recent bout of insomnia, we have all asked at least some of these questions. Perhaps we continue to secretly entertain them, even when we try to ignore them or shove them to the side. There is undoubtedly much in everyday life that encourages us to "forget" such questions as: "Why should I go on living, working, consuming when I know I'm going to die?" For example, the millions of advertising messages that we are subjected to during our lifetimes promote the fiction that the more we consume, the more we live and thus, if we keep consuming, may actually live forever! The worst advertisement would say, "Buy a Honda and feel mortal!" There is something deeply troubling and even bothersome about philosophy and its relentless questioning.

It is, nonetheless, wrong to think that philosophy is simply the repetition of the same questions. The charges of naïvety and childishness that the serious, practical, everyday world levels at philosophy come from a superficial awareness of its questions, without any knowledge of its answers. Over the history of philosophy, different philosophers have addressed the questions or objects of philosophy in different ways. They have come up with original, significant answers to the questions, and it is, above all, these answers that form the history of philosophy, enabling it to be told as a story.

There are no definitive answers to these questions, but that just means the objects of philosophy have not been exhausted. Neither have the objects of mathematics or history been exhausted. There will never be a definitive, final history of the Second World War any more than there will be a final answer to the question, "What is the numerical value of pi?" But that does not mean all those who have written about the Second World War have been wasting their time, nor does it mean that those philosophers who have dealt with the question of consciousness, for example, have been wasting theirs.

For our purposes, then, philosophers are those who have worked in the field of philosophy. Working in this field of study means they have addressed a common set of objects (or problems) and that answers to these questions follow a certain course, tell a story. The fact that there is a story implies there is continuity. It implies that those involved in the philosophical field of study take into account the accomplishments, and failures, of their predecessors.

Now, why choose some protagonists in the story of philosophy, rather than others? Why are some philosophers considered "great" philosophers? We may lay down a number of necessary conditions.

1. Great philosophers have addressed the major philosophical problems, the objects of philosophy. It is not enough to simply work on one discrete question, to the exclusion of all others.
2. They have addressed these problems in an original way; they have added something new to the story of philosophy, but at the same time, they have done this in a way that recognizes the efforts of past philosophers—even if it is to radically disagree with them. Philosophy that claims to be *entirely* original is generally naïve.
3. Great philosophers have produced a body of work. Sheer quantity of production does not, of course, signify greatness. However, a handful of journal articles or one book rarely guarantees admission into the philosophical Pantheon. As well, the body of work must be arguably coherent, a corpus where the different elements can be inter-related.
4. Their philosophies are not only relevant to us, but have been relevant to past generations of philosophers. The above three requirements usually guarantee this one.
5. Their work has enough meaningful ambiguity to have fostered generations of scholarship. There is a depth about the great works of philosophy that, in spite of all their meaningfulness, defies definitive commentary. If we completely understood Plato, we wouldn't write about him any more. Yet we must always have the impression there is something meaningful there that remains to be discovered, something greater than us, that exceeds our grasp.

6. One might say, ironically, that a necessary condition for being a great philosopher is being a dead European male. Indeed, why the history of Western philosophy has generally excluded women and non-Europeans from its narrative is itself an important philosophical question, related to the bigger object of justice. My brief story of philosophy includes a major woman protagonist and a live Canadian philosopher. This should at least show that the narrative remains open.

If I claimed that I consciously applied the above criteria, in a cold, objective fashion, in order to select my great philosopher protagonists, I would be lying. Much of the choice is based on personal taste, the simple acknowledgement that, over my personal history of study, some thinkers have appealed and spoken to me more than others, awakening in me the sense of wonderment that is present at the conception of all true philosophy. To paraphrase an important philosopher who did not make it into this account, we choose our philosophers based on who we are.

It is tempting to wonder whether we are, today, still capable of producing great philosophers with the stature of those from the past, a Plato or an Aristotle, a Descartes or a Kant. The subtext to the question is that if there are no similarly great philosophers living today, perhaps philosophy itself, as an ongoing story, is finished, having become an endless retelling of the same tale. To this crucial question, I would answer that philosophical activity has always taken place in a context, in a community of investigation where thinkers debate common questions using shared concepts. Great philosophers always arise out of such a lively intellectual community, when particular individuals seem to respond to the challenges in ways that reflect the first five of the above-mentioned criteria. In this light, maybe we can say that it is actually within a community of questioning that the essential philosophical progress takes place. There has never been as much philosophical activity, questioning and different fields of investigation as there are today. Debates in areas of ethics, metaphysics, history of philosophy, epistemology, theory of knowledge, etc., are dynamic, fruitful and global. Whether great philosophers are already working among us or whether one will come along in a year or two, in a decade or two, a century or two ... only time will tell. In any case, the background conditions are certainly in place.

A NOTE ON THE TEXT:

Throughout the book, I refer to works by the philosophers discussed. All of these works are readily available. Many are accessible electronically over the Internet; others are certainly on hand in college or university libraries or available in recent, inexpensive translations. I encourage the reader to explore the original texts I refer to throughout this story. Philosophical study does demand a special type of reading, one that requires active involvement and where re-reading is never wasted. Personally, in my own studies, I have found that the texts become more approachable and stimulating once I have acquired a kind of affinity, a certain *feeling* for the thinker and his or her thought. It is this feeling that I seek to convey, in the hope it will lead to further discovery.

1. THE PRESOCRATIC PHILOSOPHERS

T he Presocratic philosophers are considered the pioneers of Western philosophy. They are grouped together under this umbrella because they preceded Socrates, who lived from about 470 to 400 BCE. In other words, the Presocratics lived and practiced from the late 7th, into the 5th Century BCE. They also are distinct from Socrates and Plato (who, as we will see, are philosophically difficult to disentangle) in terms of the objects they addressed and the way they addressed them. The Presocratics include such names as Thales, Anaxagoras, Empedocles, Anaximander, and the two we are concerned with: Heraclitus and Parmenides

It is generally accepted that philosophy began with Thales, although we know very little about him. He apparently predicted an eclipse in 585 BCE. He was also noteworthy because, having predicted a heavy olive harvest, he bought controlling shares in the olive presses, made a lot of money and then went back to practicing philosophy!

These anecdotes show two things: the object of Thales's philosophical enquiry was nature, what the Greeks called the cosmos, i.e., the universe and all in it, including the growing season of olives. Such enquiry would today fall into the field of physics, cosmology or astronomy, but also geography, biology, anthropology, agriculture and generally every field that studies what fits into the universe. Second, the moral of the olive press story is that philosophers are capable of succeeding according to the worldly criteria of wealth and power, but they choose to be interested in other things. The philosopher is not necessarily an absent-minded eccentric, capable of nothing else; he or she is someone who consciously chooses to pursue wisdom rather than wealth.

Thales's interest in nature was typical of Presocratic philosophy, in general. The self or the human individual and God or gods are only worth considering as elements of the world. In fact, we can say that at this stage in the philosophical story the human self and God are simply particular aspects of the universal object: the cosmos. The self and God are not yet worthy of separate enquiry. In fact, the theme of the story of philosophy you are reading is the evolving relationship between the self and its world. God, as the third fundamental question, plays a determining role in this relationship, although sometimes under an assumed name (the Universe, the Absolute, the Good ...) and sometimes through a significant absence.

I want to try to give a feel for the historical context in which Western philosophy was born, and relate this to its primal interest in nature or the cosmos.

Most Presocratic philosophers did not live in mainland Greece, on the Peloponnesian peninsula, but on the periphery of the Greek world, in what might be called the provinces. Thales, for example, lived in Ionia, on the west coast of what was then called Lydia, which is today Turkey. From this coast, you look across about 100 miles of the Aegean Sea towards mainland Greece and its principal city, Athens. Presocratic philosophy is not Athenian philosophy. It pre-dates the Golden Age of Classical Greece, and the Athens of Socrates and Plato, by more than a century.

Ionia, at that time was a collection of prosperous, commercial port cities. The province only lost its predominance in philosophical, cultural matters after the Persian wars (recounted by Heroditus) destroyed those cities. Presocratic philosophy then moved to southern Italy and Sicily, and finally, much later, to Greece itself, and Athens. Thus, Heraclitus is from Ephesus, in Ionia. Parmenides is from Elea, in Southern Italy, near the Amalfi coast. The Presocratic philosophers are nonetheless Greek because they are part of Greater Greece, part of the Greek world, culture and language. What was this world like?

When we think of Ancient Greece, we have images of white stone statues, architectural majesty, white columns, symmetry etc. But, just as those statues were actually colored, Greek life was much more colorful and complex than the formal beauty of the Parthenon would lead us to believe. First of all, the cities of Ionia must have been vibrant, teeming, cosmopolitan towns, where Greek, African, Egyptian, and Persian traders mingled. And nature was colorful. Our visions of the Athenian Acropolis tend to make us forget just how close to nature the Greeks lived, particularly those who lived far from the Athenian center. Greater Greece was principally an agrarian society, and the "cities" were small. The land was rugged and almost cruel in its harshness. The omnipresent sea was unpredictable, dangerous for the navigation of the time. One can imagine the skies of this world as immense and ever-changing; the days often starkly sun-lit, the nights, unsullied by artificial light. Largely unpredictable weather changes could have huge effects on harvests and settlements.

Warfare was a fact of life, whether against the Persians, or against other Greek cities. Anyone could be called upon to fight and the fighting was bloody and merciless. If a city fell, the men were slaughtered, the women and children enslaved. War appeared as did violent weather, an unpredictable catastrophe or a joyous, blood-drenched celebration of rapine and victory. Fortunes were ever-changing and unpredictable.

Against this occasional, random savagery stood the beginnings of civic peace and prosperity, of law and order and administration. These orderly elements make the contrasting chaos and destruction of war even more shocking.

Nature itself plays out this contradiction between the orderly and the chaotic. On one hand the stars seem almost motionless or eternally describing the same orderly patterns; seasons return with cyclical regularity. Yet on the other hand, the weather brings unpredictable storms, drought and devastation.

It was Friedrich Nietzsche who, more than two millennia later, brought to light this essential contradiction in Greek character: on one hand, the sunny, reasonable, measured side of life, the statues, the columns; and on the other, the dark, joyously destructive, chaotic side. The first side, he called Apollonian, after the sun-god Apollo; the second, he referred to as Dionysian, after Dionysus, the god of wine, revelry and death. I will return to this essential dichotomy when we look at Nietzsche, later in our story. For now, I want to put forward this striking contrast as perhaps a necessary element in whatever strange brew of circumstance led to the birth of Western philosophy.

Clearly, the reflection necessary for philosophy needs more than culture, order, wealth and leisure; it also needs a strong shot of what G.W.F. Hegel will later call negativity. It is only when we are aware that the beauty of life inevitably exists on a background of always possible death, that we begin to think. Or, as the 20th-century existentialist philosopher Martin Heidegger noticed, the fundamental question is that of being itself: why is there something rather than nothing? We can only feel the power of this question, and the wonder of being, when we are conscious of its incredible lightness and fragility, against a background of not-being or death. For a graphic portrayal of this idea, we may watch again the famous scene from Orson Wells's film, *The Third Man*, when Wells and James Cotton confront each other on a Ferris wheel in a deserted post-war amusement park. Wells asserts that 30 years of internecine bloodshed among the Borgias dynasty gave civilization the cultural wonders of the Italian Renaissance, while 500 years of Swiss order and democracy gave us ... the cuckoo clock!

Both Plato and Aristotle claim that philosophy begins with a sense of wonder. Perhaps this wonderment is only truly wonderful when we are aware that what is, might just as easily not be. Whatever else went into the birth of philosophy, the Presocratic Greek world certainly allowed this sense of wonder to arise. It is almost as if humanity woke up to find itself in a strange, marvelous place, and opened its eyes to the miracle of its own almost impossible possibility.

The Presocratic philosophers find a world where things are constantly changing, coming into being and then dying away, and yet where there is also order and permanence. They are fascinated by this endless dance of chaos and order, of being and not-being, of life and death. If this child-like fascination were all there was to philosophy, however, our story would stop here, in a kind of arrested childhood. The Presocratics were not only fascinated by the miracle of being, they sought the reason for it, and this seeking for the reason is the beginning of philosophy.

To understand the newness of this "seeking the reason of things," we have to be aware of what came before. Prior to the Presocratic philosophers, the world was predominantly explained in mythological, religious terms. For the Greeks, the two fundamental references were Homer (who describes the Greek Gods and their personalities in the *Illiad* and the *Odyssey*) and Hesiod, who wrote the *Theogony*, a creation story about how the gods and the world came to be.

According to the mythological accounts, each god is an agent, responsible for the properties and workings of a specific part of the cosmos: Chaos, Gaia, Eros and others. There is no essential difference between the god and the part of the world it represents. The natural world is the revealed face of the gods. Hesiod gives his account as a story, the same way the Bible tells of the creation of the world in 6 days, or Haida myth tells of Raven releasing the first humans from a clam shell. In all of these accounts, there is no argumentation; no reasons are given. Things just are. In fact, both Homer and Hesiod begin their poems with an incantation to the Muses, the goddesses of inspiration. It is the Muses that guarantee the truth of the story, not the strength of argument or the reasons given within the account.

Using reason to explain things also divests the gods of some of their supernatural agency. They alone no longer serve as an adequate explanation for why things are as they are. Instead, the Presocratic philosophers use things within the cosmos itself to explain its workings. This is the essence of what philosophy, and that latter-day part of it called science, is about: using reason to explain things, and not relying solely on the dogmatic appeal to supernatural agents.

Awake to a miraculous world precariously suspended between stellar symmetry and earthly turmoil, the early protagonists in the story of Western philosophy asked fundamental questions about the nature of being. Why is there something rather than nothing? What is it that is, and why does it want to constantly change into something else, and strive to slip back into nothingness?

HERACLITUS

Born around 540 BCE at Ephesus, the aristocratic Heraclitus, "the obscure," had little patience for the ignorant or the vulgar. He probably witnessed the revolt of the Ionian cities in 498 BCE, and their defeat and punishment by the Persian king Darius. Perhaps this explains Heraclitus's take on war as "the father of all and the king of all."

Heraclitus wrote only one book, a long poem, *On Nature*. It should be mentioned, however, that not a single original text remains from him or from the other Presocratic philosophers. The only sources we have are the fragmentary reports and quotations from later Greek philosophers, like Plato and Aristotle. This explains why Presocratic writings appear as fragments. Such a practice shows that, over the following century, philosophy had already become a field of study as I defined it in the Introduction. There was, by the time Plato was writing, acknowledgement that the earlier thinkers had to be taken into account.

Above, I defined the fundamental problem of Presocratic philosophy as the question of being and change. How can things remain what they are and still change? Heraclitus responds to this question in a way that recognizes both permanence and transformation. Things are both what they are and what they are not, a self-contradiction that is at the very heart of being. In other words, what makes being what it is, is that it is constantly, permanently, in a state of change and transformation, driven by internal contradiction. The only thing permanent is permanent change. Consequently, as expressed in his famous epigram, reported in different fragments, one can never step twice into the same river.

The idea that things are both what they are and what they are not, that they are what they are because they are in a constant state of becoming, is difficult to express in a way that does not seem self-contradictory and it is perhaps the greatest originality of Heraclitus to have accepted that only contradictory language is capable of expressing the contradictory truth of being. Indeed, one of the striking aspects of Heraclitus's affirmations is that they are themselves as self-contradictory as the nature of being itself, and thus represent the perfect reflection of what they are meant to express.

It would seem impossible to make true statements about the things of the world if they both are and are not what they are. One falls through the looking glass into a world where reasonable language breaks down. Heraclitus attempts to overcome this problem by using contradictory statements to capture the essentially contradictory nature of the world. Thus, the affirmation about stepping twice in the same river seems to contradict itself, affirming both that the river is not what it is, because different water runs through it, while accepting tacitly that there is something constant to be stepped into twice.

We will see later how the recognition of truth as something paradoxical or contradictory (or dialectical) will push modern philosophers like Hegel, Kierkegaard and Nietzsche to follow Heraclitus in the search for new forms of philosophical expression.

Making contradictory statements reflecting the contradictory nature of being may bespeak and transmit, poetically, a deep wisdom or intuition into the nature of things, but it is not yet philosophy. To be a philosopher and not simply a mystic poet, Heraclitus must provide justifiable reasons for the permanence of change and he must do so without importing supernatural or divine agents.

Heraclitus finds the reason for change in a fundamental tension that lies at the heart of being. This tension between opposites produces change. Thus being alive is in a state of tension, like a drawn archery bow, which Heraclitus uses as an analogy since the Greek word *bios* means both archery bow and life. Being, like the bow, exists in the tension between life and death, between coming into being and falling back into not-being. Like the bow, it gives birth to the arrow's flight, although the lively arrow is ultimately an instrument of death.

In being, argues Heraclitus, there are two fundamental oppositions: 1) between identity and difference, 2) between being and not-being. These two oppositions, or conflicts, give rise to two different types of becoming or change. The opposition or tension between identity and difference produces that type of change called transformation, where things move from one state to the next. Thus my own life can be seen as in constant transformation because I am both who I am (identity) and different from who I was. I may be barely recognizable to someone who knew me 20 years ago, and yet I am who I am. If I weren't self-identical, I wouldn't change (transform). I would simply become someone or something else.

The tension or opposition between being and not-being produces generation or birth, the second type of change. How else are we to explain the coming-into-being of new things, of new things that seem to come out of nothing? How does something come from nothing? Heraclitus answers by saying that the tension between being and not-being is productive, in the same way the tension in the drawn bow produces the arrow's flight. We will re-discover this idea of productive, progressive contradiction in the 19th Century dialectics of Hegel and Marx, where again, tension produces change. In the early Greek world, the idea that destiny, movement or progress comes from within, from one's own contradictions, rather than from the determining actions of the gods, must have seemed truly revolutionary.

Heraclitus's image of the drawn bow is significant in another way, beyond the reference to the tension between life and death. The tension of the bow string may also be seen as the source of harmony, of measure and thus, for the early Greek mind, of reason. Just as bow strings of different lengths may send arrows different distances, their tension may also be conceived as a measured scale of musical notes, producing harmony. In other words, the underlying tension of being, productive of change, is also the possibility through which being makes itself heard to human understanding or at least to those with ears attuned to its strange harmonies. Heraclitus calls this truth *logos;* it is the reason, balance, measure, tension that is the law of the cosmos. It is also, the word.

The question of knowledge is an essential focus of the Western philosophical tradition. I have said that philosophy is more than wise insights. It must also provide reasons for its stated truths. However, in doing so, it must explain how these reasons can be known. It must provide a theory of knowledge. In the context of Heraclitus, it is one thing to affirm the true nature of change, as lying in the fundamental tension of being; it is another to give the reasons for change, in the oppositions between identity and difference, and being and not-being. Still further, he must show how we have access to this truth. How do we know it?

Heraclitus is very undemocratic in his theory of knowledge. The truth of being is only there for those who have the ear for its harmony, as I mentioned above, or the eyes for its inner fire, the underlying principle (in Greek, *archè*) of being and its truth.

The notion of *archè*, of an original underlying principle that is also the fundamental element or substance of all things, is crucial to Presocratic philosophy. As I said above, early philosophy is scientific rather than mystical because it seeks the reasons for things in nature itself. *Archè* is the embodiment of this task; it is both the underlying principle explaining the essence of being, and a fundamental element in nature itself. While we today may be readily sympathetic to Heraclitus's philosophical position, the idea that being is essentially self-contradictory and therefore changing, we must remember that he and the other Presocratic philosophers were scientists of nature. It was therefore not enough to explain things with purely abstract concepts, like contradiction and tension, but rather these concepts had to be rooted in a real, natural substance. For Heraclitus, this was fire, the underlying essence of all things and, as their principle, the key to the possibility of knowing them.

Indeed, when things are burnt, we experience their true essence, expressed in the uneasy tension holding together opposing elements, like air (smoke), water (vapor), and earth (ashes). Through fire, we experience the reality of their existence. Fire is seen as movement and tension and exchange between the opposites, and what unifies them.

In terms of Heraclitus's theory of knowledge, it is significant that fire casts light, and it is this light that illuminates those who are able to see the tensions at play. Perhaps we might also remark, remaining true to our first philosopher's aristocratic views, that fire can be dangerous, particularly to those who do not understand how to approach it.

PARMENIDES

Parmenides was born around 515 BCE, in Elea, in Southern Italy, inland from the beautiful Amalfi Coast. At 65 years of age, he met and conversed with Socrates, a meeting recounted in Plato's conceptually challenging dialogue that bears the Presocratic philosopher's name. Although Parmenides wrote in the epic style of Homeric verse, the most faithful articulation of his doctrine is best stated in two words: It is.

Needless to say, such a pronouncement is only philosophical if it is accompanied by some explanation and development. Parmenides's philosophy can indeed be seen as the justification of the truth of the statement that "it is." This is only possible if the "it" and the "is" have meaning far beyond what might immediately be assumed. In fact, the weight of meaning the words take on is as absolute or universal as the phrase is short. "It" is nothing less than being, the cosmos, all of nature. "Is" refers to the way it exists. In claiming that "it is," Parmenides is responding to the same question that motivates Heraclitus: what is the nature of being and how does it change? The claim that "it is," however, is a radically different response, one that disagrees with his predecessor's answer.

First, if we take the statement "it is" seriously, we see that by referring to being as "it," we are saying that being (the cosmos, nature) is one and only one. We are accepting the concept of a uni-verse, that all the diversity of nature must be thought of as One. Second, the verb "is" implies that this one thing exists absolutely. It is, means that it is not nothing. It also means it is not changing into something else, in which case, we would have to accept that "being" both is what it is and is not what it is, since it has become something else. Something else has to be seen as the not-being of what something is. So, in saying that "it is," Parmenides is affirming that being is one and unchanging, and there is nothing else.

Parmenides's justification of this truth takes the form of an elegant, valid argument form that Aristotle will later define as a syllogism (here, a constructive dilemma). It is the use of this form of reasoning that makes Parmenides a philosopher, rather than a mystic, for mystics have certainly shared this intuition of universal oneness. As is the case with all valid arguments, if you are a reasonable person and if you accept the truth of the premises, you must accept the conclusion or inference. By constructing such an argument, Parmenides is therefore not only using reason to convince; he is implicitly acknowledging the reasonableness of his audience, and the existence of a community of reasonable beings to whom philosophical discourse may address itself. The reasonable discourse of *logos* implies the existence of such a community. Whether the community of reasonable beings must be there for philosophy to exist or whether philosophical discourse creates the community in which it makes itself heard is a question we will have to leave for another time. As reasonable beings, let us return to Parmenides's valid arguments.

Proving being is one:
   Being is either divided by being or by not-being.
   If being is divided by being, it is divided by itself and is not divided.
   If being is divided by not-being, it is divided by nothing and is not divided.
   Therefore, being is not divided.
   (Therefore, being is one.)

Proving being is (unchanging):
   Whatever comes to be must either come out of being or out of not-being.
   If it comes out of being, it already is being.
   If it comes out of not-being, it is nothing.
   Therefore being is.

Both of these arguments ask us to implicitly accept the disjunction or radical alternative between being and not-being (nothingness). There is nothing in-between and there is no mixing of the two and therefore, no possibility of change and multiplicity. For change and multiplicity both require, as Heraclitus showed, the admixture of being and not-being. Things change because they both are and are not what they are. In Parmenides, the disjunction between being and nothingness is so uncompromising that it renders change and multiplicity impossible. It even appears that once we have accepted the basic premises of Parmenides's arguments, the radical separation of being and not-being, and the elimination of the latter as simply nothing, the rest of the argument is superfluous. In Parmenides's defense, however, I would simply mention that this is a feature of all deductive syllogisms. All the truth is contained in the most general premise. The rest of the argument functions more as a demonstration than as a proof. Once again, the truest statement is simply, "it is." The demonstration is there to help us see this truth.

The need for an argument or demonstration does show that the truth it conveys is not immediately obvious to all, otherwise, why bother with the argument? The need for the argument shows that most of us believe the contrary and need to be convinced of the truth: that things do not change, because there are no "things" and no "change." If this is true, our belief to the contrary must be based on illusion, specifically, the illusion of the senses, by which we seem to observe the world of many things and their transformation.

Indeed, if being is, then "our" thought is itself either being or nothing. We cannot think not-being without not-thinking or being in error. True knowledge is being and thinking what is. Conversely, error is not-being and thinking what is not. Similarly, according to most Christian doctrine, evil is not something substantial in itself that really exists, but rather the absence of godliness, which is construed as absolute presence.

The other fundamental aspect of Parmenides's thought will resonate through the Western tradition, through Plato and then through Christianity: the sensual world leads us astray. Error (sin) is not something that is there, but rather our propensity to live in illusion and not to see what truly *is*. The truth lies beyond the senses. Much of the story of Western philosophy is steeped in the rationalist belief that truth comes to us through the lights of reason, which alone can penetrate the chimera of our personal experiences and opinion.

Ultimately, for Parmenides, reason teaches us that only being is conceivable and expressible. For if error is not-being, how can we possibly say it? How can we say not-being? How can we truly say nothing? If we refer to different things and to their change, i.e., to their transformation or generation, we are referring to what is not, to not-being. We are saying nothing. So, in truth, we can neither think nor say what is not. In saying "it is," we are left with all that is true. The rest is illusion and falsehood.

2. PLATO AND SOCRATES

Plato was born in Athens around 428 BCE, into a politically influential, powerful family. He was a robust, handsome, athletic man. Athenian citizens were expected to be soldiers when the need arose, and Plato participated in the latter stages of the Peloponnesian war against Sparta and some ten years later, in the Corinthian campaign.

Plato's historical period was marked by war and political upheaval. Athens had defeated the Persians and the confederation of other city-states but had finally lost the Peloponnesian war. Sparta had installed a tyrannical government in Athens, an oligarchy (the reign of 30), which was eventually replaced with a rather messy and corrupt democracy. In spite of this upheaval, this was the golden age of Athenian culture, the flowering of philosophical, scientific and artistic activity, with the great dramatic productions of Sophocles and Euripides. Athens was a sophisticated city-state, with laws, institutions, organized politics, science and art. It was the center of the Greek world and, by extension, the centre of the Mediterranean world.

In this environment, Plato received a very cultured education and was destined for a political career. However, he seems to have become disenchanted with this option through the disreputable actions of some of his own powerful relatives, members of the ruling oligarchy of 403-404 BCE. Plato visited Italy and Sicily when he was around the age of 40, and became lastingly, and disastrously involved in the politics of the city-state Syracuse. Plato founded the Academy, in Athens, around 388 BCE, near the sanctuary of the hero Academus. Some have called this school the first European university, referring to its teachings of mathematics, astronomy, physical sciences and philosophy.

After a final trip to Syracuse, where he attempted and failed to draft a constitution based on the political ideas of his own philosophical dialogue, the *Republic*, Plato returned to Athens and continued his work at the Academy, until he died in 348 or 347 BCE.

Philosophically, Plato's early influences were defined by Heraclitus and Parmenides, and, above all, by his own teacher, Socrates, who was sentenced to death by the Athenian parliament. Plato was present at his teacher's trial, but was absent at his execution, when Socrates drank the poison hemlock. Plato's philosophical dialogues the *Apology*, the *Crito* and the *Phaedo* are poignant accounts of Socrates' trial, his reflections on death and the immortality of the soul.

Plato inherited much from his Presocratic predecessors, Heraclitus and Parmenides: a faith in reason as a means to knowledge; the distinction between rational truth and opinion; the idea that the senses may lead us astray; a belief in *logos* or reasonable discourse as a way to true knowledge. However, Heraclitus and Parmenides also left Plato with two equally appealing and yet deeply contradictory visions of being: the vision of the cosmos as the unchanging One, versus a universe where nothing is constant but change itself.

In fact, this dilemma is typical of our story of philosophy. One philosophical protagonist is faced with a problem (object, question) which he or she will answer in an original, coherent way, leading to an advance. However, this advance will raise further challenges that must be confronted by those who follow.

Besides their conflicting theories of the nature of being and change, Heraclitus and Parmenides left Plato with a problem that strikes at the core of philosophy and the possibility of *logos*. When taken to their limits, the thoughts of each of our two Presocratic philosophers seem to render impossible the reasoned discourse upon which philosophy and science depend.

Reasoned discourse requires statements of predication, where a grammatical subject is related to a predicate through a verb, usually the copula "to be." We must be able to determine and affirm that a thing *is* something if we are to convey any sort of knowledge. Iron is a metal. Water is a liquid at room temperature. Humans are mammals etc. However, in a world where things are constantly becoming something else (Heraclitus), statements that affirm the truth about the way a thing *is*, are ultimately false. If the Mississippi River is never what it is from one instant to the next, I cannot even identify it as the Mississippi River. Even the most essential form of predication, identifying something as itself, is impossible. And how can I say that iron is a metal, if I cannot even say that "iron is iron"?

The same problem arises, but in a different way, in Parmenides. If all I can truthfully say is that "it is," any statement that claims a thing is something else is false. I cannot say iron is a metal because the statement involves predication between two different things, and all is One. In fact, I cannot even truthfully say that iron is, because naming a thing "iron" implies it is itself a separate thing and there is only One. I want to show how Plato's teacher, Socrates, helps him reconcile the problems posed by his two important predecessors.

SOCRATES

The most important influence on the young Plato was Socrates. In spite of his importance, it is very hard to sum up Socrates philosophically. He wrote nothing and so his ideas are largely transmitted to us through dialogues that Plato wrote, where Socrates appears as a character, and through other accounts of his time. The degree to which Plato's literary creation of the character is faithful to the real Socrates or rather acts as a mouthpiece for Plato's own ideas is disputed. In any case, to the extent Western philosophy considers Socrates as a founding father, it is founded on an ambiguous figure whose actual thoughts remain a matter of debate!

We do know that Socrates's origins were humble: his mother a midwife, his father a stone cutter. Socrates did not posses Plato's patrician bearing. Unlike his most famous student, he was apparently ugly and short, with a snub nose. He was, however, a distinguished warrior, and, in his deep respect for the laws and customs of Athens, a perfect citizen. Sentenced to death on dubious charges of corrupting the youth and impiety, he refused the opportunity of escape, since it would have meant breaking the law and living in exile.

In spite of his apparently Bohemian behavior (he was not given to pursuing the fixtures of wealth and power), and while he managed to create many enemies for himself among the politically powerful, he remained a member of the intellectual and artistic elite of his city. In that context, he certainly got invited, or invited himself, to the best dinner parties, where, if we are to believe Plato's account at the end of his *Symposium*, Socrates's appetite for wine was only matched by his inexhaustible ability for sober-minded philosophical discussion.

Philosophically, I want to present Socrates through three main characteristics.

1. Unrelenting enquiry. All previous knowledge must be questioned, particularly that of his philosophical predecessors. However, Socrates was also unrelenting in interrogating his fellow citizens and especially those who claimed to possess certain knowledge of anything at all, regardless of their rank. A favorite target for his relentless questioning were the Sophists, a group of thinkers who charged money for instruction in various practical areas of knowledge. This constant scepticism and irreverence towards those in power or in-the-know was rightly deemed dangerous to the established political order and eventually led to Socrates being charged with corrupting the Athenian youth, and sentenced to death. Upon being condemned, at the end of the dialogue the *Apology*, Socrates provides an elegant, valid argument proving that death cannot be bad. However, his unrelenting enquiry causes him to doubt even this comforting conclusion. Thus, to the essential question of life and death his final answer remains, "Only God knows."

2. Socrates was a man of words, but in a very specific sense. Rather than writing long poems or dissertations, Socrates used dialogue as a means to attain the truth. *Logos*, the reasonable discourse, is possible, but only in dialogue form, involving another

person. Dialogue is not a casual conversation. It is no "talk show." Socratic dialogue operates like a scientific instrument. The technical term for the process is *elenchus*, where a series of definitions are put forward by the participants, discussed, and refuted or accepted with reservations so that a further, more accurate definition may be put forward, and so on until, hopefully, the truth is arrived at.

3. Socrates, immersed in the vibrant social life of Athens, is more interested in the human world than were the Presocratics. He inquires into questions of virtue, justice, truth and the good, not as they play themselves out imperfectly in the world, but as pure essences. The eternal, unchanging nature of such essences makes them worthy objects of philosophical consideration. As we see in Socrates's speech from the *Apology*, after he is wrongly condemned to death, true justice may be impossible in the world, but that should not stop us from seeking to know what it is, in essence.

Socrates's influence allows Plato to reconcile the conflicting worlds of Heraclitus and Parmenides. First, regarding the problem of philosophical discourse that arises when we attempt to express a cosmos in perpetual change or a static universe where all is One, Plato finds a solution in the dialogue form invented by Socrates. After all, a philosophical dialogue involves both the Heraclitean aspects of tension, conflict and movement, as well as the Parmenidian aspects of permanence. For the object of the dialogical enquiry can only be something essential and unchanging, like the true nature of virtue, or the good or justice. But, as a form of discourse, the dialogue is more of a process than an argument. Through the often opposing affirmations of the participants, the dialogue both says what things are and what they are not, gradually eliminating the different, faulty statements, in order to leave us with the truth about the object sought.

Plato also shares with Socrates the belief that the human world must become the object of science. After all, Plato lives in the intensely political atmosphere of Athens. Socrates allows him to see that while human activity is in constant flux and chaos, philosophical inquiry deals with the permanent essences that form the underlying substance of the world. These essences are unchanging and universal in nature, the same way mathematical/geometrical objects are meant to be unchanging and universal.

The philosophical question is "how can we know the perfect essences if they don't actually exist in the world?" If worldly virtue is always imperfect, for example, how can we possibly know true virtue? How can I experience it? What is it? Where does it exist if not in the world? Plato's solution is a theory. It is both a metaphysical theory and a theory of knowledge: it is called the theory of Ideas (or Forms).

Metaphysics literally means "beyond the physical," beyond the natural world we live in. It is an important dimension of Western thought, where reasons for things are found beyond the realm of the apparently physical universe. Although later philosophers, like Nietzsche, might disagree, this is not the same as the religious, supernatural thought we find in Hesiod. We are not, in metaphysics, saying: things are this way because the gods decreed it so. Metaphysics attempts to find the reasons for things through concepts, principles and finally, through reason itself. For example, stating that God exists and using this statement as a premise in an argument is religious. Proving that God exists, as a conclusion to an argument, is metaphysical. Plato's theory of Ideas is a metaphysical theory that explains the existence of the essences of things beyond the physical world using concepts of reason.

Plato's theory of Ideas is also a theory of knowledge, perhaps the first, in that it explains, coherently, how we can know the truth of things, in this case, the essence of things beyond the world of the senses. Theory of knowledge, like metaphysics, is an ongoing, important field of philosophical enquiry.

For Plato, the essences of things that we can investigate philosophically, the objects of philosophy, are unchanging Ideas or Forms. In a way, they can be thought of as perfect models for the imperfect things of the world, for all the worldly, incomplete instances of virtue, beauty, justice etc. The essences or Ideas transcend the objects of the world. They go beyond the things of this world and yet, at the same time, are present in the (imperfect) things of the world. There is a perfect Idea of a horse, for example, which is the essence of all worldly horses, making them what they are, although each example never attains the perfection of its essential Idea of "horseness."

Plato's Ideas are not subjective, personal or abstract, as we generally think of ideas today. The Ideas or Forms are in fact more real, more objective than the things of the world. They are the real essence and substance of the world. The world only participates in or partakes of these forms. So, where are they?

It is tempting to say, they are "out there," beyond, in heaven etc. However, the idea of a realm floating above us, full of real Ideas, makes little sense and renders the theory rather implausible. Perhaps we can say the Ideas are "beyond" in the same way the big monotheistic religions think of God as being beyond. If we describe God as infinite and universal, He is both beyond us and present in us. He is out there but also always here. In philosophical terms, Plato's Ideas, like God, are both immanent and transcendent. In Christian terms, for example, we might say God is present in a human act of charity, but the act is not God itself.

As a theory of knowledge, Plato's theory of Ideas relies on the notion of knowledge as a process of recollection. Plato puts forward the hypothesis that the human soul, or mind, does not perish with the body. Rather, after death, the soul dwells for a time among Ideas. Subsequently, it is reincarnated in a body. However, before birth, the soul crosses the river of forgetfulness, *Lethé*, and so is reborn having forgotten what it has witnessed among the essential Ideas. In coming to know what virtue or beauty is, then, we are recalling what we once knew. Plato recounts this hypothesis in a literary form similar to a parable or a myth.

This may seem shocking when measured against the reasonable demands of *logos*. In Plato's defense, I would argue that science always has its limits, beyond which current best efforts are incapable of grasping. In response to these limits, science has always come up with metaphors to temporarily fill the gaps in its knowledge, allowing science to carry on its inquiries. Thus, the metaphor of a Big Bang, helps us grasp the ungraspable creation of the universe, just as, in the past, the idea of an ethereal element that transmitted waves of light helped us get on with science until we could conceive of quantum theory. Plato's theory of recollection is a metaphorical creation allowing him to hypothesize about the human soul and the nature of mind.

The theory of recollection explains how essential knowledge (of the objects of science/philosophy) is within us, is inborn. It explains how learning universal truths is actually a process where we give birth to the knowledge within us. In his dialogue, the *Meno*, Plato has the character Socrates show that essential geometrical truths are within us and that well crafted demonstrations simply bring out this knowledge or make us aware of it. We recognize the truth when we see it.

To make this understandable, it may be helpful to remember what sort of knowledge Plato is really after. We are not trying to know factual bits of knowledge, things that can be memorized like dates or recipes or skills. The objects of knowledge are rather the unchanging, eternal essences of things. We can all relate to this. Although we may not be able to define justice, beauty or virtue, for example, we certainly believe we can recognize instances of them when we see them. Even children seem to have an innate feeling for "fairness," though they have not thought it through. Who could dispute that we immediately recognize that a square divided diagonally in half will give us two equal triangles, or that two parallel lines, on a two-dimensional plane, will never meet? If perfect justice is no more present in the imperfect world than is a perfect square, our knowledge of these things, these Ideas, must be inborn, in our souls or our minds. Further, if the soul/mind carries these Ideas within itself at birth, it must itself have experienced them somewhere before birth. Therefore, the soul must exist beyond birth and death. Plato's use of a myth form to present this theory is indeed highly metaphorical. However, when today's neurologists and psychologists refer to "hardwiring" in order to explain how we seem to have an innate grasp of grammar that enables us to quickly learn a mother tongue, they are simply using a new metaphor to attempt an explanation of the same phenomenon Plato encountered.

☞ Plato accepts the distinction Parmenides makes between opinion and knowledge. Opinion may be useful, and derived from what we see or hear, but it cannot attain to true knowledge, which is defined as justified true belief. However, the greatest difference between opinion and knowledge involves not so much the learner's experience in apprehending objects, as the nature of those objects themselves. Some objects can only give us knowledge in the form of opinion. True knowledge involves objects that are eternal, unchanging essences. I can know that one line bisects another line at one point only, whereas knowing who the queen of Egypt is, will always be a matter of opinion, even if that opinion involves the highest degree of likelihood. Knowledge, for Plato, always involves knowledge of the Ideas and therefore relies on our soul's experience when it is not incarnated. Although Plato admits there are Ideas of such lowly things as mud, this implies that our truest knowledge of them can only be of their mathematical nature, in much the same way that today the truest knowledge of the deepest, smallest physical entities is best expressed in mathematical formulae.

As humans, it is our task to aspire to true knowledge, to approach wisdom. The philosopher has an erotic love or desire for wisdom, a *philo* (love) – *sophia* (for wisdom) that pushes him or her upward to the highest object of love: the good. Philosophy, like worldly love, is neither rich nor poor. It is somewhere in the middle, possessing enough knowledge of the object of its desire to know what it is missing, and therefore to have the desire to seek it. The reference to desire shows that philosophy is not a sterile, academic pursuit but rather the highest form of love or, which is the same thing, love of the highest Idea.

It is true that the highest form of Platonic love is non-sexual. We may refer to a "Platonic love" between individuals. However, in Plato, this does not mean that desire for human beauty is morally bad. Sexual desire is merely a stunted and arrested desire. It is a desire to know a worldly, finite, imperfect object (a human body) that will ultimately change and decay, rather than something eternal and unchanging, like Beauty itself. Ideally, the desire we feel for earthly beauty should stimulate our desire to know the actual form of Beauty, and what is most beautiful is the Good. The highest form of love is knowledge of the Good and knowledge of the Good is wisdom.

This idea of a hierarchy of love, depending on its object, is far removed from our modern, romantic, self-centered ideas about love. For Plato, the highest love itself is not beautiful; it is love of the Beautiful. The highest love is not true; it is love of the True. The highest love is not good; it is love of the Good.

In his monumental dialogue, the *Republic*, Plato uses a cave analogy to describe the education of his ideal State's political leaders, the philosopher-kings. Plato asks us to imagine a prisoner chained, with others, in the depths of a cave, attached in such a way that they can only look onto the rear wall. On this "screen," images are projected by puppeteers who, while themselves hidden behind a low wall, hold up various objects and puppets so that the light of a fire behind them casts shadows on the wall. Into this realm, a liberator comes, who frees the prisoner and leads him up to the mouth of the cave. The prisoner's eyes are painfully opened, first to the light of the fire and finally, to the brightest light of all: the sun.

The analogy describes the ascent of knowing, from false opinion, up to the highest Ideas. Significantly, however, it also describes the duty of the initiated philosopher (the former prisoner) to return to earth and to put his knowledge to effect in a politically just State. Opening one's eyes to the truth is a painful experience, a gradual apprenticeship that involves first recognizing that what we have taken for reality is, in fact, illusion, a shadow-play projected on the wall of the cave. When we struggle up to the sun-lit mouth of the cave, the world itself (the realm of the Ideas) is so blinding, we must first accustom ourselves to its brilliance by observing only its reflections on water (representing the study of mathematics). Finally, we may open our eyes to the *real* world (of Ideas) and, briefly, to the sun itself (the Idea of Ideas, the Good).

The pain of this eye-opening is, however, nothing compared to the philosopher's subsequent fate. He is pulled back into the cave, where, still blinded by the former brilliance of the truth, all is now darkness. Further, he is incapable of carrying on normal conversation with his former mates, the cave dwellers. He sees that they are really talking about nothing. He is awkward and ungainly in this new darkness. He appears ridiculous to the others, delusional dwellers of the illusory "real world." This was perhaps Plato's own fate, drawn from his disastrous attempts at producing a just State in the Sicilian city of Syracuse. Or, perhaps we may refer to Baudelaire's reference to the albatross, a bird whose broad wings are majestic in flight but ridiculous when it is forced to waddle about on the ship's deck.

Most people would probably blanch at the idea of a State run by philosophers, of philosopher-kings. Today, we seem to prefer technicians, businessmen, lawyers. However, if we take the word "philosopher" as it was meant, as a lover or seeker of wisdom, and we understand wisdom as knowledge of the Good, who could possibly want to be ruled by anyone other than "philosophers," by those who seek to know the Good?

Perhaps most importantly, for the development of our story, Plato introduces the truly revolutionary idea of the soul as something transcendent, existing beyond the worldly realm of the body. This immortal substance is not yet the Christian soul and certainly not the modern notion of selfhood we will discover later. Plato sees the human soul as something we carry within us that transcends our earthly individualities. The soul is ours and yet not ours. It animates us and yet is most at home beyond us, in the realm of the Ideas, with things of a similar substance or nature, and particularly, with the forms of the Good, the True and the Beautiful. Such a soul must aspire to its lost home, and perhaps, if we are attentive to it, it may carry us, philosophical apprentices, with it in its aspirations. Plato invites us to acknowledge that we possess within us something approaching perfection and eternity and that carrying such a precious thing, for our brief time between birth and death, is a great responsibility. We must cultivate our soul, certainly not sully it and, if possible, leave it, when we die, better than when we "found" it. In this sense, Plato presents his teacher Socrates as dying the philosopher's death, sure of at least one thing: that it is better, for the soul, to submit to an injustice than to commit one.

3. DESCARTES

ARISTOTLE AND THE MEDIEVAL SCHOOLS

In Plato, we discover something new within us, something transcendent that connects us with the possibility of wisdom, with knowledge of the Good, the True, the Beautiful. Having come across this notion of the self as soul, it is tempting to leap ahead to the next defining moment in its story, the invention of the modern concept of selfhood, which we discover in the 17th-Century philosopher, René Descartes. We would thereby leave Plato and the Ancient world in 4th Century BCE and skip over the following 2000 years. The reader, however, would be justified in wondering about a story that leaves out so much, particularly when I initially presented the story of philosophy as a field of study where the protagonists take into account what went before, either building on it or reacting against it, or both.

In order to present Descartes and his vision of modern selfhood, we have to understand the philosophical context in which his philosophy takes place and what it was reacting against. Descartes is often considered, in the field of philosophy, to be the originator of modern philosophy. To understand why his thought is modern, we have to understand what came before, what it took into account and how it was so revolutionary.

If we had to assign one philosophical figure to the 2000 year period between Plato and Descartes, we could safely propose Aristotle, as well as the Christian interpretation of his philosophy in Medieval or Scholastic thought. This is certainly not to say that Plato has been forgotten. Besides his direct influence on Christian thinkers like Augustine, Platonic thoughts on the real existence of ideas, the immortality of the soul as the transcendental seat of the Good in humans, innate knowledge, the dialectical nature of truth, and the power of reasonable argument have become permanent acquisitions in the gallery of Western thought. The story, however, does not stop there.

Aristotle studied at Plato's Academy and was private tutor to Alexander the Great, a position where, given his master's lust for conquest, he truly got to see the world. At the Academy, he learned Plato's theory of Ideas/Forms, the metaphysical theory that explained the cosmos and human knowledge of it. This doctrine is primarily what Aristotle reacts against. Perhaps that is because Aristotle is far more interested than Plato in the actual things of the world, not just in their essential or ideal truth but in all their chaotic multiplicity. Aristotle seems to have written about everything he encountered, plants, animals, political systems, art, language, the stars, morals and the history of philosophy. In fact, it is largely thanks to his writings on his philosophical predecessors that we have a fairly accurate representation of Presocratic thought.

It might well have been Aristotle's curiosity about the rich diversity of the world that lead him to question the Platonic theory that worldly things are nothing but the shadows of the transcendent Ideas, which are supposedly where the real truth lies. At the same time, Aristotle does accept the traditional belief, first discovered in Parmenides, and embraced by Socrates and Plato, that science must concern itself with essences, with the underlying, unchanging substance of things. So the dilemma facing Aristotle is, how do we come to know the things of the world as more than shadows or illusions and still seek their essences? In other words, how can we find the essence of things, that which does not change, not in the transcendent Platonic Ideas, but in the things themselves, when these things themselves seem to be constantly changing?

Aristotle's solution is to attribute something like a soul to all individual things and a soul to all living things. Such a soul is not to be confused with the Platonic human soul, the immortal part of us, at home in the realm of the Ideas. It is the essence of a thing, that which makes it what it is or, more accurately, that which makes a thing do what it does. We might say, to use Aristotle's analogies, that the soul of the eye is to see; it is vision. Or, the soul of an ax is its ability to cut, its "cuttingness." Similarly, the essence or soul of a plant is its ability to grow. The soul of an animal is its ability to move itself. The soul of a human is its ability to think. In all these cases, the soul is what animates a thing to do or be what is essential to it.

Most importantly, however, the soul is not some inner nucleus or other-worldly substance, but the actual form of the thing, not "form" in the Platonic sense of "Idea," but form as we understand it today, as morphology, as the observed shape of something. Thus, the soul of the eye, as vision, would give the eye its actual worldly form (lens, pupil, retina etc.) The soul of the ax would be its cuttingness or the form of its edge (without the edge, the ax becomes a hammer). The soul of an animal is the form enabling it to move itself (moving skin, legs etc.). The human soul (an animal that thinks and lives politically) is present in the actual self-propelling, upright, speaking, brainy form of the human being. We may say that Aristotle takes Plato's "Form" and brings it down to earth, where we can now investigate the essence of something or understand its soul by observing its actual form.

Aristotle's idea of the soul as actual form enables him to know things by observing and classifying them according to their shapes, initiating the scientific practice of morphological observation and classification that stretches well into the 19th Century when it is supplanted, in the life sciences, by advances in chemistry and genetics. Aristotle's theory is very successful in explaining the diversity or multiplicity of worldly things. The question remains, however, for a philosopher interested in the actual stuff of the world, how does this idea of essential form account for change and movement, which Heraclitus had identified as a constant feature of the cosmos? Relegating change and movement to the realm of opinion (Parmenides, Socrates, Plato) is simply not good enough for a philosopher like Aristotle, who believes that observing what things do actually tells us something true about what they are.

To explain movement or transformation, Aristotle's revolutionary idea is to distinguish between potentiality and act. Potentiality is a thing's ability to change, but to change in a certain way, according to what it actually is or what it is in act. We tend to think of the word "act" as itself a movement. For Aristotle, however, it is best to think of act as the final resting position or actualization of things, having become what they are. The potential of the thing is its movement to the point where it becomes what it really is. Things become, through their potentiality, what they are in act. For example, a seed is the potential of the tree, whereas the tree is the act or the actualization of the seed. It is this act or actualization, this final form of a thing, that drives the movement through which the seed grows into the tree. The final form is what animates the movement of the seed into becoming what it really is in act, the tree.

It is thus apparent that the tree is the final true form of the seed and the animating force of its movement. Above, we already saw how a thing's true form was its soul. Now we see how that true form also determines the movement or becoming of the thing. The actualization of a thing is its soul or essence. Things can be seen as actualizing what they really are by moving to an end point which is their purpose or their soul. Their essence is their end or purpose, and also the principle of their movement/change. It is their motor. Consequently, we can understand change as essential, since things that become are moved by their essence or their soul which is their final form or purpose. Further, we can observe and know this essence in the form that things become.

Observing the world around us, we see constant change. Beings are incessantly in frenetic movement, becoming what they are, then dying away. As Heraclitus noticed, the only constant seems to be change itself. When we raise our eyes to the night heavens, however, we are struck by a whole realm of objects that hardly move at all or seem to move with a circular regularity that escapes the logic of potential and act. In cyclical stellar movement, every point is both final and a new beginning, both potential and act. In fact, the further away we look from the earth, the less movement there appears to be. Beyond the stars, must not there be some place of absolute rest, some point that does not move at all, some being that is fully actualized, towards which all else moves? Must there not be a point of universal accomplishment that is the source of all potentiality and movement but is itself absolutely unmoved? According to Aristotle's theory, without a final point of rest, there can be no movement. Therefore, the very fact that we can observe the worldly movement of the cosmos proves the universe has a point of absolute actualization that is the source and final form of all becoming. Such a point of absolute act, such an unmoved mover, writes Aristotle, might be called God, the first and final cause of all else. Further, if, as Aristotle claims, all knowledge is knowledge of causes and if the first and final cause of everything is the unmoved mover we call God, then are not we saying that all knowledge-seeking science aims at knowledge of God?

Aristotle's science, his theories of soul, movement and the cosmos were rediscovered by Western Europe in the 12th Century, through contact with the Medieval Arabic thinkers, Averroës and Avicenna. Influenced by them, the Catholic philosopher Thomas Aquinas demonstrated that reason and faith could co-exist, particularly if reason was founded on Aristotelian science, and its pursuit of the final cause (God). There is therefore nothing heretical about *proving* the existence of God, for that is what all science ends up doing. Aquinas's elegant proofs of God's existence are therefore presented as so many "ways" to Him. At least one of these ways explicitly reproduces Aristotle's proof: If there is movement in the world, then there must be a prime, unmoved mover. There is movement in the world. Therefore, there is a prime mover. Let's call this God. This compelling, systematic vision of the universe came to be embraced and sanctioned by the Church of Rome. It provided the way the world was understood until the Renaissance of the 15th and 16th Centuries.

This is the scientific world Descartes is born into, a world where the essences or souls of things determine their behavior, their ways of becoming and moving. Science consists largely of identifying these essences through the classification of different species of things according to their actualized forms. While such classification involves empirical observation and primitive experimentation, the ultimate goal of philosophy is to discover the first and final cause, and thus to prove the existence of God or to reconcile Christian theology with Aristotle's science. Yet even here, in medieval philosophy, in the desire and the belief that any individual thinker can, through reason, prove the existence of God, we recognize the audacity of Greek *logos* and the liberating scientific spirit that will come to the fore in the Renaissance.

DESCARTES

René Descartes was born in 1596 in La Haye, in the Loire Valley. The Europe of that time was a patchwork of rival principalities and states fraught with religious strife between Catholics and Protestants.

At 10 years of age, precocious Descartes entered the Collège Royal de la Flèche, which he described as one of the most famous schools in Europe. Here, he studied what can be called a classical curriculum: the Roman (Latin) classics (Cicero, Virgil, Horace), philosophy and logic (Aristotelian). Ethics were taught, with examples from ancient Greek and

Roman history and literature as well as physics and metaphysics, much of which consisted of commentary on Aristotelian texts. Run by the Jesuits, the college embodied the happy reconciliation between Catholic faith and Aristotelian knowledge that had characterized the late Middle Ages. The Jesuit tradition of openness to science meant the teachers at the Collège de la Flèche remained relatively open-minded to such revolutions as Galileo's discovery of the moons of Jupiter in 1610, an event celebrated at the school and condemned by the Church. Galileo's discovery confirmed the Copernican theory that the sun and not the earth was at the center of the cosmos, spelling the end of Aristotle's scientific vision. Such a powerful and lasting (18 centuries!) vision does not go quietly.

Descartes took a law degree at the Université de Poitiers, thereby exemplifying the eternal flirtation between the philosophical and legal vocations that stretches back to Socrates's ambiguous tussles with the Athenian sophists (the equivalent of latter-day lawyers) and Plato's own brush with a sophistical/political career. Indeed, many figures in the Western philosophical tradition have studied law, usually at the behest of a strong father-figure, only to abandon it for the erotic desire for wisdom. Of course, countless thousands of unknown lawyers have moved in the opposite direction, from philosophical studies to a more lucrative vocation in law. They, however, are not part of this story.

In 1618 Descartes moved to Holland, to the military school of Maurice of Nassau, Prince of Orange, where he learned the arts of swordplay and riding. Descartes apparently found no contradiction in fighting as a Catholic for the Protestants in several military campaigns, and then later engaging in military campaigns for the Catholic Duke of Bavaria. Perhaps his scientific interest in the mechanics and design of military machinery allowed him to rise above such rivalry.

After two years in Paris, living as a gentleman, fighting duels, discussing philosophy and writing, he moved back to Holland. Torn between his inherent sociability and his desire for solitary contemplation, he spent the next two decades moving from town to town. In 1637, he published his ground-breaking *Discourse on Method*, and four years later, his famous *Meditations*. Both texts are published in French rather than in the academically standard Latin.

In 1649, he was invited by the philosophically gifted Queen of Sweden, with whom he had been engaged in a fruitful philosophical correspondence, to come and live at her court, as a kind of royal philosopher. Unfortunately, the Queen insisted upon meeting Descartes for philosophical discussions, on horseback, in winter and very early in the morning; we can only assume that the combination of early rising and the Swedish cold contributed to his death, a few months later, in February, 1650. Descartes had always abhorred early rising and some of his greatest philosophical insights apparently came to him while lazing in bed.

Descartes was a philosophical revolutionary. He is often considered to be the initiator of modern philosophy, primarily for his fundamentally new conception of selfhood, but also for his radical overturning of philosophy as it had been practiced previously, and which he had learned at La Flèche. Much of what his education had taught him seemed very questionable or debatable. The knowledge presented was based largely on authority (e.g., if Aquinas says it, it's true), personal opinion and tradition. The only thing that seemed really solid was the mathematics he had learned and particularly Euclid's geometry, as found in his *Elements*.

Euclid's geometry introduces basic, fundamental postulates or axioms on which the entire system of plane geometry rests. For example, all right angles are equal; a straight line can be drawn by connecting any two points. From the basic principles, one can develop further propositions, such as, a triangle contains three angles totaling 180 degrees; a square divided on its diagonal produces two right-angle triangles etc., thus allowing the subsequent development of complex propositions like the Pythagorean Theorem.

Descartes was fascinated by the Euclidian method of geometry. The fact that from a few, self-evident principles, one could deduce and construct an entire system of science seemed to promise the possibility of a universal mathematics, a type of true, certain knowledge radically opposed to the confusing hodge-podge of opinions served up at La Flèche. Rather typically, the idea of a universal mathematics actually comes to Descartes as a revelation or a dream, in bed. Perhaps, he reasoned, such a universal method could not only be applied to all natural phenomena, to the position and movement of planets or earthly objects, but to any area of knowledge. Any problem may be solvable if we reduce it to its simplest elements, the ones that are best known (like Euclid's postulates or axioms), then gradually build on this foundation, adding propositions that are true by inference until the solution is reached. In the *Meditations*, Descartes applies this method to the three traditional objects of philosophy: the soul, the world and God. Almost as a byproduct, he comes up with the invention or discovery of the modern idea of the self.

On one level, this invention occurs in the philosophical discourse (*logos*) itself. In the first of the *Meditations*, we are immediately struck by the insistent presence of the first person singular pronoun. This is new and unsettling for those who have only been familiar with Ancient and Medieval philosophy, where the "I" is missing. Plato, for example, never speaks to us directly in the first person. He writes dialogues where his thoughts are either generated in the "dia-logos" (double discourse), or he puts his thoughts in the mouth of his literary creation, Socrates. Aristotle writes from a disembodied, scientific perspective. His discourse presents the truth from an objective, not a subjective point of view.

Medieval philosophy embraces scientific objectivity as the manifestation of Christian humility. The scholar is a self-effacing compiler of previously accepted knowledge. In this context, it is right that scientific discourse take place in Latin, a universal technical language that belongs to the scientific community, without actually being anyone's mother tongue. Perhaps most significantly, the footnote is invented, whereby the veracity of the discourse is founded on numerous references to an objective, generally accepted body of knowledge. The medieval notion of scientific objectivity is still recognizable in many scientific fields today, particularly in the "hard" sciences, the ones that rely on a mathematical discourse, but also in "softer" sciences. For example, fields like political science, psychology and sociology usually base their truth claims on the objectivity of their "research methodology." The subjective point of view is synonymous with opinion and arbitrariness.

Into the universe of scholastic objectivity comes Descartes, who not only publishes in his own mother tongue, French, but uses the first person singular. In fact, the first person singular "je" appears seven times in the first sentence of his *Meditations*! Such language not only introduces the subjective individual into philosophical discourse, it opens up the possibility for any "I" to participate in Descartes's meditations. In other words, the use of "je" not only recognizes the individual subjectivity of the writer, but solicits the engaged selfhood of each reader, who can see him or herself in the open "I" of the *Meditations*. This recognition of individual selfhood is deeply liberating, as anyone reading the work cannot help but feel.

As well, in Descartes's use of the first person singular, we feel a new and engaging timeliness in his *logos*. Rather than striving to reflect timeless, even eternal truth, detached from any sense of time or space, Descartes's *Meditations* are firmly situated in the here and now. We are invited into his intimacy, into his chambers, where, by candlelight and in his dressing gown, he deduces the self, the world and God. By implication, anyone may embark on a similar voyage of contemplation and discovery, at any moment and anywhere. I may do it here and now, regardless of where and when I am.

This personal voyage begins with a kind of distillation of the self, a rejection of all that is extraneous to me and my own thoughts. Such a recovery of the individual self involves the radical doubting of everything that I have previously learned about the world, of all that has been taught on authority, of all the shifting, cloudy, confused knowledge that I have been made to accept. It is with such radical doubt that Descartes begins his *Meditations*. According to the universal method, inspired by Euclid's geometry, true science must be based upon the simplest, most certain principles, building from there. To discover these, we have to doubt all the other baggage we have acquired. In fact, we must doubt everything in order to see if we can discover something, some element of certainty on which to ground our pursuit of knowledge.

Such an extreme position of doubt is called skepticism (*skepsis* = Greek for doubt). Doubting everything usually leads to a kind of philosophical tailspin, with no possibility of recovery, which, in its purest form, can be expressed in the nihilistic mantra: nothing is true; even if it were, we could not know it; even if we could know it, we could not communicate it. Far from being nihilistic, however, Descartes's skepticism is motivated, mature and free.

Descartes's skepticism is motivated by science and the search for truth. It is a constructive element in a scientific method devoted to discovering the truth. Even if no foundational truth is discovered, his doubt still acknowledges the possibility of finding out that nothing is certain, which is itself a truth. It is akin to Socrates's knowledge that he knows nothing, as the first step in the path to true knowing.

Descartes's skepticism is mature in that it means doubting knowledge that has already been painstakingly acquired or learned. It is not an immature, lazy, puerile doubt that saves one the bother of learning anything.

Most importantly, Descartes's radical doubt is a fundamental expression of modern, individual freedom: as a self, I am free to doubt. In fact, freedom to doubt everything lies at the core of what it now means to be a self.

In his first meditation, Descartes is faced with a methodological problem: how to doubt everything without examining each and every individual thing in turn, a process which would take up far too much time and energy. Since everything he has learned has been learned through the senses, Descartes concludes that a convenient way to doubt everything would be to doubt the senses themselves as the source of knowledge. In fact, what I learn through my senses strikes me as the most certain. So, if I show they are doubtful, everything becomes doubtful. I will thus have doubted everything, and perhaps, then, I will see if anything remains certain. Descartes comes up with four hypotheses to test the certainty he has in his senses as the source of knowledge.

1. Madmen think they perceive things that they don't. Perhaps I am mad. If I am mentally deranged, I cannot be sure of what my senses tell me. Descartes immediately dismisses this hypothesis. The fact he is not mad is, to him, self-evident. Why? Perhaps the activity of reason is enough to banish madness. The madness hypothesis is discarded because if it were true, the whole enterprise of founding a universal science on certain truths would itself be mad. This, for Descartes, is impossible. Therefore, I cannot be mad. The hypothesis of madness cannot throw my sense knowledge into doubt.

2. When I sleep, I cannot be sure I am awake or dreaming. Perhaps I am asleep and dreaming that I am experiencing things that I am not. However, even if I'm dreaming, I still dream of images of things that must exist in general and that I have experienced through my senses. I may dream of a winged serpent, but I can only do so because I have witnessed, through my senses, things with wings and others that are serpents. Dreams do not throw my sense knowledge into doubt.

3. What if God is deceiving me? What if God were the author of all my impressions, making me believe I perceive things that are really illusions? However, God is perfect by definition. He is the fountain of truth. Error is what God is not. If I am in error, it is my fault, not God's. God cannot be a deceiver. Therefore, the idea of God the deceiver cannot throw all my sense knowledge into doubt.

4. But what if there were an evil spirit, not God, who is constantly deceiving me, making me think that everything I perceive is real, when it is an illusion? I cannot refute this hypothesis as I can the others. There is no way I can prove this isn't so. Consequently, imagining there is some evil spirit that constantly deceives me is enough to throw all my sense knowledge into doubt. This hypothesis successfully leads me to doubt everything that I perceive as existing. This means all my knowl-

edge of, or acquired through, external sources is doubtful. This is the case because all we are required to do is come up with the smallest doubt about the sensory source of our knowledge. The hypothesis of the deceiver may not appear likely but I cannot prove it is not so; therefore it is enough of a doubt to throw everything I have learned (in school, in the world, from masters etc.) into uncertainty and doubt.

Descartes admits that holding himself in this skeptical position is tiring, a kind of self-imposed insanity. It is far easier to fall back into the slumber of illusion, to believe the truth is just what I know of the external world, through my senses. As in Plato's cave, it is easier to keep staring at the wall, sure that the shadows are reality, than it is to look at the light. It is so much easier not to question things, to take things as they appear to be, to fall back to sleep.

Descartes's all-embracing skepticism, however, is tied to his scientific method of finding elements that are intuitively certain, and then building on them. The intuitively certain elements are clear and distinct to the mind, two qualities that are the ultimate criteria for true knowledge in Descartes. Truth is not the correspondence between externally observed facts and our ideas. This is now impossible, since all our external observations have been thrown into doubt. Rather, the truest ideas are the ones that appear to us as the clearest and most distinct, just as the founding principles of Euclid's geometry do not have to be demonstrated or proven, because they are perceived by the mind as immediately and clearly true. It is impossible to doubt them when we reflect on them carefully.

Descartes's first certainty, the axiom that he discovers after doubting everything he experiences through the senses is simply that "I exist." The idea is that even if I deny that I have external senses, and even if I deny that I have a body, it is still I who do the denying and persuade myself of this fact. Even if there is some great deceiver or evil genius who deceives me about everything, it is still I who is deceived. As Descartes writes in his second meditation, "He can never cause me to be nothing as long as I think I am something.... I am, I exist each time I pronounce it or I mentally conceive it."

Having discovered this element of certainty, that he exists, Descartes then enquires into what he is. He first attempts to define himself in an Aristotelian way, seeking to define his essence: Men are reasonable animals. I am a man. Therefore I am a reasonable animal, but he quickly abandons this as too difficult and tedious. He would have to define "animal" then "reasonable," then prove that he is part of this genus and species. Man has "little time and leisure," writes Descartes, acutely aware what a luxury it is to have time to think. Let's not waste the time we do have. So, in an attempt to figure out what he is, Descartes methodically divides himself into two parts: the body and the soul.

First, the body. Descartes defines this in geometrical terms: the body simply occupies space and has a certain figure. Can he be sure he has a body? Descartes refers back to the great deceiver who has thrown all sense knowledge into doubt, and answers no.

What about the attributes of the soul? Descartes is not concerned with defining the essential nature of the soul, as Aristotle would do. Instead he concentrates on the activities of the soul, which for Descartes include all that "animates" the body, gives it life: movement, feeding, sensation and thinking. Most of these activities are involved in the body, however, and are only perceivable through the doubtful senses. The only activity of the soul that cannot be separated from the existing I is the mental activity of thought. I know that I think and I know it immediately in a way that is absolutely clear and distinct. I cannot know that I am, that I exist, without thinking that I am. To know I am is to think I am. As Descartes puts it, I exist, that is certain, but how often? Just when I think. I am a real thing and really exist, but what thing? I am a thing that thinks. Whether or not we subscribe to the formal logic of Descartes's argument, it is hard not to be seduced by the massive intuition it provides of personal selfhood.

In fact, what Descartes has done is define the modern idea of the self. More accurately, he has defined the self as consciousness. To be a self is to be conscious of one's selfhood, to take oneself as an object of reflection, to be able to affirm, "I think that I am. I am a thing that thinks (it is)." This idea of the self as self-reflecting, or reflecting on itself, or as self-consciousness is what Descartes means when he writes: "I know that I exist, and I inquire what I am, I whom I know to exist." In other words, the inquiry into the nature of the self is the nature of the self as consciousness. I am not conscious if I am not conscious of my self, and I am not a self unless I am self-conscious.

It is important to grasp what Descartes has in mind when he defines himself as "a thing which thinks." He is not talking about a computer, a thing that only computes or calculates. When he says "a thing" he merely means an existence, something that exists, or a something. Thinking is defined first and foremost as mental self-inquiry, and then in a very broad sense, beginning with doubt and including such mental activities as affirming, denying, willing, refusing, imagining and feeling.

We can now sketch out Descartes's epochal invention or discovery, the modern self. It is immediately associated with the activities of the mind. It is also immediately associated with consciousness, with self-reflection or self-awareness. Crucially, the self is also immediately associated with the freedom to doubt. Perhaps we can also say that the new self is implicitly mortal. As conscious, self-reflecting thought, it is conscious of the "little time" life affords to thought, unlike Plato's idea of the soul, which does its best thinking after death.

Now having reached his one certainty, the certainty that he exists as a thinking mind, Descartes turns to the things of the world, to see what he can know of them. He does this because, as something that thinks, he also has thoughts of bodily things, and he cannot prevent himself from thinking that he knows these things, tested by the senses, better than he knows himself, although he admits this is strange. Should we not naturally better know the thing with which we are most intimate, namely ourselves? Nonetheless, Descartes decides to investigate the world of "other things." He chooses, as an object of experiment, something that is close at hand, a piece of candle wax. He has immediate experience of it through his senses, and therefore, he should know it best. If he can't know something this perceivable, how can he know other bodies?

Descartes says that what, on first reflection, he appears to know of the wax, he knows through the senses. He describes its taste: sweet with honey. He describes its odor: the flowers from which it was drawn by the bees. He describes its color, its shape or figure and its size, even the sound the hard wax emits when it is struck by a finger. Thus we know this body called wax through the senses. Now, continues Descartes, we approach the hard wax to a flame. All its sense qualities change. The taste and odor evaporate. It changes form and no longer emits a sound when struck. Its color changes.

So what remains of·the original wax? How do we know it is the same substance we have before us now? Perhaps Heraclitus was right. We cannot bathe twice in the same stream, and therefore, neither can we know it.

This is not Descartes's position. He maintains that when we remove all the changing sense impressions that an object may provide us, all that remains is pure extension, something occupying space that can take on different forms, different flavors, different sounds, odors etc. However, these perceptions are not the thing itself. I therefore cannot know the thing through the senses, or the "imagination," as Descartes calls them. I can only know things through reasoning or judging or understanding, through my mind's eye, one might say. My thinking judgments may be clear and distinct or cloudy. If I say wax has extension as a body, occupying space and that this body can take on an infinity of qualities, then I have a clearer and more distinct idea of wax.

For Descartes, this is the ultimate essence of the wax or of any other worldly body. This is their substance: pure extension, occupying space. Therefore, the clearest, most distinct ideas I can have of bodies is geometrical. Geometrical extension is the essence and substance of material things. The truest knowledge we can have of worldly things themselves is their geometrical position and shape.

This view of the world, as pure extension, devoid of any color or characteristics, whose essential truth is best captured as points and lines on the Cartesian geometrical plane (with its x and y axes) is certainly bloodless and impoverished. All the more poetic or romantic ideas that we have come to ascribe to nature are thoroughly absent in Descartes's world. His notion of objectivity is a soulless clockwork robot, a mechanical creation devoid of any inner life or expression. Perhaps this is because all living, spiritual qualities have been appropriated by that massive, modern creation, the self. The self is free to doubt the world. In fact, the self comes to exist through its doubting of the world, its rejection of the world as something radically other than itself. Perhaps a self-reflecting, free, doubting self can only be itself to the extent it is not all the rest. However, this also leaves the rest (the world) strangely devoid of selfhood.

Descartes's brilliant invention has this unfortunate side-effect: to the extent the self is real and substantial, it cuts itself off from everything else. To the extent the self is subject, all else becomes object. Even other "selves" are, from the point of view of myself, ultimately experienced the same way I experience other forms of extension, either through my sensory imagination or through geometrical judgment. When Descartes describes his uncertainty as to whether the caped and bonneted figures passing by his windows are really selves like the one he has deduced as himself, and not mechanical robots, he is describing a type of alienation bordering on the pathological.

To the extent we have inherited fundamental aspects of Descartes's free, doubting, self-reflective notion of human subjectivity, we have also inherited this self-ish, two-faced view of the world, where each of us feels him/herself to be the center of a universe that is devoid of all truth other than that which we can instill in it. The purely objective world, which includes our own bodies, tends to become something foreign to our inner selves. It is there for us to understand, to determine, to manipulate, to assimilate, to modify, to improve, to use.

The holistic vision of the Presocratic philosophers, living and thinking unencumbered by the Cartesian self (or the Platonic soul), implies a sense of oneness with the cosmos, a sense that the same rules that govern nature hold sway in the human being. We may, today, yearn nostalgically for this lost sense of belonging to nature. However, accomplishing such oneness must either involve abandoning our modern notion of individual self-awareness and freedom or interpreting it in new ways, something the rest of this story will perhaps help us do.

4. HOBBES

nglishman Thomas Hobbes lived at the same time as Descartes and like him, was faced with a brave new world of scientific discovery, one that had largely rejected the centuries-old domination of Aristotle, in favor of the sun-centered cosmos of Copernicus and Galileo. Dealt a hand of conceptual cards so similar to the one held by Descartes, it is striking how differently Hobbes plays his philosophical game. This is particularly evident regarding each philosopher's view of the self, in its relation to the world.

Thomas Hobbes was born in 1588 in Westport, and studied at Oxford from the age of 15. His father was a clergyman who abandoned the young Thomas to be brought up by a wealthy uncle. At Oxford, Hobbes studied much the same thing Descartes had studied at La Flèche: a classical curriculum of Latin, Greek and Logic (Aristotelian). He responded to this dated Scholastic "learning" much the way Descartes did, by looking for a new foundation for knowledge.

Following Oxford, Hobbes became a private tutor for the son of a wealthy aristocrat, Lord Devonshire, remaining close friends with his student throughout his life. Hobbes actually died at the Devonshire estate in 1679, at 91 years of age.

With his student, Hobbes traveled frequently to France and Italy, where he met Mersenne, and other Cartesians, as well as Galileo. At the age of 40, Hobbes discovered the *Elements* of Euclid. They inspired him much as they had Descartes, awakening the idea of a method for science that begins with the simplest elements and then makes inferences from them. Hobbes's main works *De Cive* (On the Citizen) and *Leviathan*, appeared in 1642 and 1650, when Hobbes was around 60 years old, demonstrating that, unlike athletes and movie stars, philosophers can produce their best work later in life, thus providing hope for legions of aging philosophy professors.

Hobbes's earliest published work (1629) was a translation of the Greek historian Thucydides. This is significant for two reasons. First, Thucydides, as a Greek writer of Plato's time, is very un-Platonic. He recounts the actual worldly dealings of the politics of power at the time, the speeches in the Agora, the intrigues, the battles, the slaughters. He describes in wonderful detail the workings of the City-State and the players involved. Second, Thucydides's book is called *The Peloponnesian War* and recounts the war between Athens and Sparta. This was essentially a war within the Peloponnesian peninsula, within the Greek empire and may be viewed as a civil war between two cities, with two systems of belief. Hobbes's interest in Thucydides already reveals what will become for him a dominant philosophical concern: civil war, war within the State, the war of citizen against citizen.

The concern with civil war is amplified in a much less theoretical way when, in 1640 civil war actually breaks out in England, between Cromwell and the forces of Charles I, and Hobbes has to flee to France because of his perceived royalist sympathies. He only returns in 1651. While in Paris, he writes his Objections to Descartes's *Meditations*, which were shown to Descartes anonymously by their mutual acquaintance Mersenne. Apparently, Descartes didn't appreciate the criticisms. Most of the controversy between Hobbes and Descartes centered on questions of physics. Although both refused the Aristotelian conception of matter or nature, where shapes and movements are determined by the formal soul, potentiality and act, Hobbes had a radically different solution to the problem of worldly substance than did Descartes.

We have seen how Descartes reduces matter to geometrical figure and location within a substance whose characteristic is extension. Hobbes's inspiration in physics is derived directly from Galileo's laws of mechanics, and specifically from his theories of motion, inertia and gravity. Rather than explaining movement as an inherent quality (act) of a body itself, as Aristotle had done, Galileo presents it in terms of force. Put simply, bodies continue at rest unless force causes them to move; bodies continue moving unless force causes them to stop. This means that there is no *essential* difference between rest and movement. Rest is simply a special state of movement. The static weight of an object, for example, is an impeded movement toward the center of the earth. This is a radical departure from Aristotle's theory, whose main principle was that a body (other than God) cannot be both in movement and at rest. While Descartes was also inspired by Galileo's mechanical vision of the cosmos, his idea of extension is essentially static. Hobbes, on the other hand, adopted the dynamic idea of the cosmos in various but constant states of movement. One thing Hobbes does share absolutely with Descartes, however, is a belief in the Euclidean method: science must begin with the simplest, best-known elements.

Hobbes's thought can be approached through these two fundamental ideas: civil war and motion. His interest in civil war translates into a concern for human affairs, political affairs, and the question of human community. His central question is, how can humans live peacefully together? How can we avoid war within the human community? In answering this question, Hobbes's method is Euclidean and his ontology (vision of how things really *are*) is Galilean.

Rather than begin by stating, as Aristotle observed, that "man is a political animal," Hobbes seeks the conditions of possibility for human social interactions. In order to do this, he must first consider the most basic element, i.e., the human individual, and then, given the nature of this element, deduce how it can be a social or political animal. We cannot presuppose that man is a political animal. Only by starting with the individual human can we understand how he or she can live in civil society, can be a citizen among other citizens within a state. The human individual is the Euclidean element with which we must begin our investigation. Once we have understood this element, we can infer how it might interact with other similar elements. So, we must begin by answering the question, "what is man?"

In order to discover the essence of the human individual, to understand individual selfhood, Hobbes does not adopt a uniquely meditative, introspective approach. Nor does he begin from an original, metaphysical question about whether things really exist, as Descartes had done. This approach would seem suspiciously Continental, and simply contrary to good English common sense. Besides, if the cosmos is governed by the universal laws of motion and inertia and the human being is part of this cosmos, then this being must also be determined by these laws. Why should the human individual escape the laws that govern everything else in the universe?

Of course, by putting things this way, Hobbes has already refused that thing which is most central to Descartes's vision of the self: the fact that, as a free, doubting mind, the self is an exception to the laws of nature. Hobbes sees no reason to subscribe to such an ethereal substance as mind, something which cannot be empirically observed and which somehow makes its own immaterial laws. The universe is made up of material things, obeying the laws of motion, and the human mind is no different. It must also be a material thing, explained in terms of motion and inertia.

Thoughts are thus material things, derived empirically from the senses. Sense objects exert a pressure (movement) on our sense organs, causing a corresponding movement in our nerves, to our brain, and then to our heart. Here, there is a kind of wave of resistance that is set up through the blood. In other words, we experience a reaction, a feeling about what we have perceived. For example, color and light is a movement that strikes our eyes, setting up an internal movement that runs along our nerves to our brain and then to our heart, where we have a feeling of what we have experienced. The sight of an apple, when we are hungry, awakens a feeling of appetite. We may think of the process as a series of billiard balls striking one another and conveying a movement along their line. There is no essential difference between the billiard balls outside the mind and those inside. The mind is a continuation of natural law and occurrence. However, our minds are clearly more complex than this simple stimulus-reaction model allows for. How does Hobbes explain such thoughts as memories or imaginings, or the discursive thought necessary for constructing arguments?

Just as a moving object tends to continue its movement, by inertia, a physical sensation tends to continue its movement within us, as a thought or a mental image, over time, even though the actual stimulus is no longer present. This explains memory. The movements we perceive continue internally, as memories, gradually fading or slowing as they encounter resistance, finally stopping in forgetfulness. Discursive thought, which allows us to construct sentences and arguments, is explained by the fact that thoughts or images string themselves together in "trains of thoughts." The logic of these trains of thought, what brings separate thoughts together, is simply desire, either for material things, for sexual purposes, or for glory. These passions animate the individual and can be thought of, themselves, as internally generated movements.

With regard to passions, humans are no different from animals. What does distinguish humans is their ability to reason and use language. For Hobbes, the two are inseparable. To reason is to use language. Language is the external movement of reason, which, in turn, is the continuing movement of our thoughts, brought together in trains, according to our desires and ultimately derived from our perceptions of external, natural movements. If language is ultimately what separates man from animal, it is simply because the human is an animal that uses language.

Hobbes's theory of language, as a distinct subject of philosophical enquiry, is original and modern. According to him, language is a system of signs or names that we assign to things, a view that anticipates 20th-Century semiotics, the study of language as a system of signs. The idea of separating the sign from the thing it signifies is revolutionary. For Hobbes, the fact that language can be considered a system of signs means it is not essentially different from mathematics, another system, which uses different signs. Most importantly, the similarity between language and mathematics means that reasonable thought can be explained as a type of mental calculation that uses word signs instead of number signs. Thus, we can judge the truth of a proposition by evaluating whether the subject is equal to the predicate. "A three-sided figure (subject) is (=) a figure with three angles (predicate)" is true because subject and predicate are equal.

We may say that, for Hobbes, reason is essentially material and calculative. It is very much like a computer, using verbal signs instead of the computer language of 1's and 0's. However, rather than being a disembodied thinking machine, the human mind is part of a passionate animal driven by desires. What the mind therefore calculates is how the human individual can best satisfy them. In other words, reason is to man as claws are to the tiger, or teeth are to the shark. It is an instrument enabling him to get what he wants.

This vision of the "self," if we can call it that, is very different from Descartes's. Hobbes's vision of the individual mind is materialistic, naturalistic and deterministic. That is to say, the mind is determined by the same laws that determine nature, the mechanical laws of motion and inertia. Personal freedom is, therefore, extremely problematic.

Having defined the simplest element, the human individual, Hobbes can now derive an answer to his question about how humans may live together peacefully. However, since the human animal is essentially known as a hungry, calculating animal, a kind of de-fanged, thinking shark, the question becomes especially pressing. How can this self-ish, hungry animal get along in civil society?

To explain, Hobbes performs what might be called a thought experiment. He imagines what would happen if his elements, the individual human beings he has discovered, were simply brought together in a kind of primitive condition he calls the State of Nature. Hobbes is here not claiming to make an anthropological or paleontological discovery about the actual conditions of primitive humans. In fact, he explicitly writes that he is not at all sure whether such a condition ever existed (although he does refer, in passing, to the "savages" of North America). His intention is to write political science, based on certain elements and the inferences drawn from them.

Hobbes's first inference is therefore that, given his definition of the human individual as entirely natural, as only determined by nature, this is what natural human society would look like: selfish, hungry, calculating individuals pursuing their own interests. Thus, the state of nature, described in the *Leviathan*, is a state of constant warfare, of man against man, of civil war, where every individual is incessantly fighting for survival and the things necessary for his or her survival. There is no account of history, no arts, no literature, no communal society and people live in continual fear of violent death. The life of man in such a condition, writes Hobbes in a particularly pithy expression, is solitary, poor, nasty, brutish and short.

It is interesting that Hobbes bases his state of war not on difference, but on equality. It is not because people are different, nor because the stronger ones dominate the weaker, that there is strife. Rather, it is because everyone has relatively equal strengths and weaknesses that there is conflict or "civil war." Otherwise, the strong would simply rule and impose a state of equilibrium or peace. This is not the case in the state of nature, which is defined by unrest and conflict.

The problem is, if humans are motivated by selfish desire, what reason could they possibly have for putting an end to the state of nature and forming civil, peaceful society? Hobbes's solution is to make a distinction between a right of nature and a law of nature. The right of nature (or natural right) of the individual is to do everything in his power to preserve his life. Natural right is limitless. It gives every individual the right to everything, even to other people's possessions, and bodies, in order to preserve one's own life. In its limitlessness, the right to survive quickly becomes the desire to over-survive, to have everything.

On the other hand, the law of nature is described as a precept or general rule "found out by reason" which forbids a human from doing that which would be destructive to his or her life. As derived from reason, the law of nature is therefore the result of a calculation. Hobbes shows that natural right is actually contrary to natural (reasonable) law. This is because living only according to natural right actually produces conditions that are contrary to natural law, since those conditions are actually destructive to human life. The state of nature is the embodiment of such conditions, where humans live only according to natural right. Here, one lives in constant fear of immanent death.

The law of nature, by which man can do nothing that is self-destructive, therefore becomes: man must seek peace in order to preserve himself. He must therefore be willing to "lay down" his natural right, for peace. However, he may do so only if others are also willing to follow suit, otherwise he would be contravening the law of nature and exposing himself to danger. So, motivated by self-interest, in order to preserve one's life, human reason calculates that it is best to follow the law of nature. Further, we do this in order to best accomplish the right of nature, to get what we want and preserve our lives.

Ultimately, the goal is comfortable living, in peace, without fear of death. Hobbes thus provides us with a pioneer expression of that fundamentally Anglo-Saxon, value system that underlies much of what is known as the American Dream, where the middle-class desire to live ever more comfortably and at peace has become an ethical end in itself. The fact that such a purpose may appear to be perfectly obvious to us only signifies that we have largely adopted this ethical end over alternative views, like social justice, religious devotion, valor, domination, truth, ecology ...

In Hobbes, however, what is to prevent someone, or some group from breaking the natural law? What is to prevent someone from taking advantage of the fact that all the others have surrendered their natural right? Hobbes's answer is that, in order to obey the law of nature, all individuals have made a covenant or a pact by which they have surrendered or, more accurately, transferred their right. In other words, the citizens have made a social contract by which they have transferred their rights to one supreme individual (or small group) called the Leviathan. This individual is literally empowered by such a massive transfer to become a "mortal god," a kind of nuclear compression of all the natural rights which have been transferred to him (or to her) by the multitude of individuals.

The Leviathan is not a tyrant, nor someone who has seized power, since the citizens have freely surrendered their rights to him. Citizens are not alienated by this transfer of right, since their rights have not been taken from them. The Leviathan is simply a living expression or representation of the public's general will, an actor whose role is determined by all those who, in contracting with each other, have written his script. He is all-powerful, but only because the multitude has empowered him. We can thus see why Hobbes' theory was not popular with royalty, who ruled by divine right and not by a popular contract.

In exchange for the massive transfer of right he has assumed, the Leviathan must ensure the peace and safety of the multitude. Although the transfer or right is absolute, and cannot be taken back, the Leviathan has the implicit obligation to maintain peace. This obligation to respect the transfer of power is strong because failure to ensure peace is not in his interest. The resurgence of natural right (and civil war) among his subjects means the Leviathan may be removed or killed. It is easier to assassinate a dictator than a majority. The sovereign must therefore be sufficiently powerful to ensure that no one reclaims his natural right and breaks the law of nature.

The Leviathan's power is derived from fear. Fear is the passion that motivates, or moves humans into a commonwealth and keeps them there. No one breaks the contract, simply because everyone fears the consequences. Fear of death is a fundamental human motivator. It causes humans to seek peace. It causes them to maintain peace by neutralizing the only other essential human passion: the limitless desire to survive, where survival means always desiring more.

Hobbes's view of the self and its world is pessimistic. There is no reference to a free, doubting, self-reflecting mind that is able to stand opposed to the mechanistic laws that determine the natural universe. Humans are moved by exterior circumstances or by internal motivations that can always be reduced to two basic passions: fear of death or desire to possess. Reducing the self to such a level seems to imply a repressive political structure, one that sees the human individual as just as nasty, ugly and brutish as the natural state that occurs when he is left unrestricted.

We may certainly recognize the ghost of Hobbes in such contemporary political expressions as our constant fear of crime and terrorism, and the accompanying acceptance of more law enforcement and stronger, more constraining laws, as well as in our endorsement of longer prison sentences for criminals, or in our ready acknowledgment that we need stronger armed forces, more discipline at home and in schools, etc. We may now even understand these expressions as resulting from a certain (pessimistic, materialistic, mechanistic) view of the human soul. Perhaps the most important lesson learned from Hobbes's political thought, however, is the idea that, in the final analysis, we get the government we deserve, that without the massive, voluntary transfer of right, the Leviathan is nobody and nothing.

As consolation, no matter how far we find ourselves defined simply by our fears and desires, we can never be entirely Hobbesian. It is only part of who we are. The Platonic soul and the Cartesian self are not easily forgotten, and nature itself kicks against its reduction to purely geometrical extension, to the laws of motion and the mechanistic workings of a clockwork world.

5. ROUSSEAU

Although Descartes and Hobbes choose differing philosophical approaches to the question of selfhood, each nonetheless leaves us with an incomplete and unsatisfying picture of how their creations are related to the world, to nature or, to use a more technical term, to objectivity. For Descartes, the objective world is ultimately reduced to points and lines on the geometrical axes; for Hobbes, nature is a mechanistic creation, following the pre-determined laws of movement. Each of these truncated views of the world reflects poorly on the self that it implies: Descartes's self tends to be excessively self-ish and solipsistic, cut off from everything but itself. Hobbes's self is a slave to the deterministic laws of nature, and devoid of any personal freedom. The thinking of Jean-Jacques Rousseau reinvigorates the relation between the self and nature, thereby giving new life to each.

Rousseau is an ambiguous philosophical personality and consequently, he is difficult to define. Part of the difficulty lies in the non-systematic nature of his philosophy. Rather than relying on the deductive method observed in both Descartes and Hobbes, where inferences are drawn from axiomatic certainties, Rousseau brilliantly employs the more literary forms of the essay, the novel, the dialogue and autobiography. Regardless of the ambiguous aspects of his thought (or maybe because of them!) his contribution to the modern idea of the self and its world is profound. Without Rousseau, the history of Western philosophy would probably appear to us as someone else's story, where we would not entirely recognize ourselves.

Jean-Jacques Rousseau was born in Geneva in 1712, and died in France in 1778. His life falls squarely into the cultural, historical period known as the Enlightenment. This period is characterized, generally speaking, by a confidence in human reason, seen as the liberator and savior of mankind. There is a fundamental belief that the spread of knowledge can cure humanity of its ills, most of which are attributed to ignorance, either in

its pure, innocent form or as promoted by obscurantist religious dogma. Ruling monar-
chies were generally seen as complicit in the promotion of ignorance, through their support of either Protestant or Catholic ecclesiastical structures.

The belief in all-powerful human reason was already apparent in Descartes, who is
able, through its sole use, to deduce himself, the world and God. Even Hobbes, although
his definition of reason as calculation is radically different from Descartes's, participates
in its unprecedented promotion; a law derived from reason (natural law) saves mankind
from an eternal state of nature and civil war.

In France, in the 18th Century, a group of thinkers, *Les Philosophes*, embodied the
designs of the Enlightenment, carried out through the incredibly ambitious and optimistic *Encyclopedia* project. The idea was to get the best minds of the day to write, in a universal language (French) an encyclopedia of all human knowledge, which would thus be
accessible to anyone. The spread of knowledge would contribute to educating and culti-
vating individuals, society and mankind as a whole.

Our own universal system of public education is based on this belief, that knowledge raises us up, liberates us, makes us better and thereby contributes to the betterment
of humanity. Today, this core tenet of our state-supported education systems often enters
into conflict with more practical, job-training aspects and the belief that productivity,
rather than knowledge, is the panacea for humanity's short-comings. This contradiction
is apparent in how we view another modern-day expression of universal knowledge: the
Internet. Seen as a system of universally accessible "knowledge" (without distinguishing
between knowledge and information), the Internet appears as the continuation of the
Enlightenment's *Encyclopedia* project: the idea of a knowledge-based world as a means of
social improvement. However, it is also promoted as a production/consumption-enhanc-
ing tool.

Rousseau was a regular contributor to the *Encyclopedia*, as were the other
Enlightenment figures Diderot (its editor), Voltaire, and Holbach.

However, even as they were writing or editing their monumental, 35-volume work,
which was begun in 1751 and only completed in 1780, the main participants were becoming disenchanted with their own original idea that knowledge alone can cure social ills.
Such disenchantment is reflected in Voltaire's novel, *Candide*, through the ridiculous
know-it-all character, Pangloss. It is, however, particularly true of Rousseau, whose profound questioning of the Enlightenment provides much of the basis for his tremendous
influence on Western thought. His questioning stems from a conviction that, far from
curing human ills, reason may actually be responsible for causing many of them.

Rousseau was the son of a Geneva watch-maker and was apprenticed to an engraver
at an early age. He rebelled against this form of indentured servitude and left Geneva,
beginning a period of wanderings and adventures that included employment as a servant
in Turin, Italy. Perhaps his unfortunate experiences as an apprentice and a lackey gave him
a feeling for social injustice and an aspiration for freedom. Perhaps his refusal to enter the
watch-maker's world can be seen as striving to embrace a more organic, less mechanistic

view of nature. In any case, the rebellious Rousseau was fortunate in being taken under the wing of a wealthy French aristocratic lady who provided him with the necessary leisure for studying, reading, writing and learning music, at her estate.

Rousseau actually became an accomplished composer and produced a fairly successful opera. He corresponded with the *Philosophes* and, in 1750, wrote his *Discourse on Sciences and the Arts*, which won an essay competition held by the University of Dijon. The essay gained him widespread notoriety. Four years later, he published his *Discourse on the Origin of Inequality Among Men*, and, in 1762, he published *The Social Contract* and *Emile*. As a reward for these philosophical achievements, Rousseau found himself officially condemned by the Archbishop of Paris, blacklisted by Rome, censured by the Sorbonne, banished from Switzerland, and in dispute with the *Philosophes*. He took refuge for a short time with the Scottish philosopher David Hume, before the two fell out, and lived the remainder of his days in lonely, paranoid misery. His *Confessions* and his *Reveries of a Solitary Walker* were published in 1780, two years after his death.

The main question Rousseau addresses concerns the nature of human ills. In spite of their vast differences, both Hobbes and Rousseau seek an end to what the former referred to as "civil war," conflict between citizen and citizen. Similarly, both philosophers further their inquiries by imagining a state of nature, which is meant to reveal something essential about human nature. Here, however, the resemblance ends. A fundamental difference arises from their conflicting views of what that nature is. For Hobbes, humans are nasty creatures, driven by hunger and fear. Civilization implies the domination and control of these passions. Rousseau, on the other hand, sees man as naturally good. Civilization has mainly served to degrade him from his originally happy and harmonious condition.

Already in his first work, his *Discourse on the Sciences and the Arts*, Rousseau questions the Enlightenment idea that civilization and the universal spreading of knowledge lead to a better human condition. In fact, in that writing, civilization is seen as decadence, a moral degradation. The barbarian is superior to the civilized Greek. The martial Spartan is superior to the decadent, civilized Athenian, and Roman decadence begins with the importing and learning of Greek science.

The same theme is further developed in the *Discourse on the Origin of Inequality*. Here, we find a description of a state of nature radically different from what we find in Hobbes. Rousseau's state of nature resembles earthly paradise, before the fall from grace. The human individual lives a solitary, happy life in the virgin forests. Humans live in harmony with nature, like healthy animals, without sickness or disease. There is a perfect balance of natural needs and satisfactions. Natural man is not driven by passions of pride and desire, as Hobbes had affirmed. There is no reason to have these passions since humans are solitary and satisfied.

The state of nature is not a state of civil war, of every man against every man, as Hobbes had said. As Rousseau writes, war is not natural to humans. "War is not a relation between man and man, but between state and state." Further, war is the result of inequality. In the state of nature, all men and women are equal and therefore there is no strife, a conclusion radically opposed to Hobbes, for whom natural equality is the original condition for human conflict.

Above all, for Rousseau, in the state of nature, man is free. This is the same as saying that humans are naturally free. Natural freedom means freedom from the authority of other humans. In such a state, there are, of course, constraints but they are entirely natural, i.e., the conditions of nature that humans have to deal with: hunger, thirst, procreation, cold etc. These natural constraints are not seen as impediments to our original state of freedom, simply because they are natural rather than man-made. Only humans can suppress the freedom of other humans.

In Rousseau's state of nature, there is no fire, no tools, no reasoning or language. Humans may meet and mate. They stay together as long as necessary to nurture their offspring, which isn't long since nature provides abundantly, then they separate again. Far from being driven by the powerful Hobbesian passions of fear and hunger, the only natural sentiment, for Rousseau, is pity. A human who sees another human (or animal) injured, feels pity. This is the natural passion, a gentle passion. Natural man is naturally good.

This state of nature is not a myth, and Rousseau stresses this, but rather a historical hypothesis, based entirely on conjecture, not on anthropological facts (although we can observe the rather fanciful anthropological figure of "le bon sauvage" at play here). By stripping away all that comprises civilization, we are able to see what the natural human state looks like. As well, the state of nature hypothesis allows Rousseau to see civilization itself as a cumulative process that gradually removes the human being from what it is naturally. Thus, Rousseau can claim that his state of nature reaches further back than Hobbes's, revealing a condition prior to any human society, even one that is in a constant state of conflict. This historical dimension also allows Rousseau to describe plausible stages of the progression from the primitive state to more civilized ones, something Hobbes fails to account for.

The historical progression Rousseau describes is not a necessary human evolution. Man does not naturally improve or evolve into something better and more civilized. The so-called progression of human history is entirely accidental. It could just as easily not have happened. This means that civilization is an accident, or rather a series of accidents or catastrophes that befell the natural human being. This is a crucial point, since otherwise civilization would be a natural thing in humans, as in Aristotle, where man is defined as an essentially social animal. For Rousseau, civilization must remain unnatural, even anti-natural.

A series of natural disasters force humans to become social animals. First, a period of long droughts and cold winters force individuals to band together, forming temporary, wandering herds of hunters and gatherers. This is no longer the state of nature, but a savage state, where nature no longer immediately supplies all human needs. Further natural calamities, floods and earthquakes, force humans to establish permanent, yet rough settlements, without laws, where vanity, pride, jealousy arise. Here, at a level of civilization akin to Hobbes's original state, fear of revenge is the only thing that keeps humans in check.

It is again, as Rousseau puts it, "an unhappy circumstance" that forces humans out of this primitive social condition: the molten rock from catastrophic volcanic activity leads to the human invention of iron, along with the workable plowshare and agriculture. Far from being seen as a crucial step in the development of human society, the invention of agriculture is particularly unnatural since it causes the holistic earth to be cut up into separate properties belonging to different individuals or groups. This is the first cause of civil society and inequality. "The first person who built a fence around and stated, 'this is mine' and found others simple enough to believe him, founded civil society."

From now on, society is divided into those who have and those who have not, into rich and poor. In order to protect what they have, to prevent robbery, the rich make laws to maintain the peaceful status quo. This is the basis of the much vaunted rule of law that characterizes modern, civilized societies. Laws, claims Rousseau, are there to give more strength to the strong and more shackles for the weak. Laws destroy, once and for all, natural freedom by institutionalizing property and, hence, inequality.

Thus, we understand what Rousseau means when he writes, "Men are evil ..., however man is naturally good ... What can have depraved him to this point if not the progress he has made and the knowledge he has acquired?"

This is a revolutionary idea in every sense of the word. Thinkers of the Enlightenment had believed exactly the opposite: that humankind could progressively improve itself, raise its condition through reason and knowledge and civilization. Rousseau is saying exactly the opposite: reason, knowledge and civilization are the sources of inequality and evil. The idea is also revolutionary in a political way, since it implies that the status quo is unnatural and unjust. If humans are naturally free, then the unnatural state of civilization has deprived them of their freedom. Rousseau's famous statement, "Man is born free and he is everywhere in chains," would inspire the 18th-Century democratic revolutions in America and France. It is no wonder the thinker was ostracized by the powers of both Church and State. Rousseau, however, does not advocate political revolution. His proposed solutions to injustice and inequality are far gentler and more reasonable, revealing the less obvious Enlightenment side of this ambiguous philosopher.

The problem is, if civilization and progress have brought us to a point where we are living in an unnatural, evil condition of inequality and bondage, how do we find a solution? How do we remedy this condition? Rousseau recognizes the impossibility of a return to a state of nature. Although much of the 1960's back-to-the-land nostalgia can be seen as reminiscent of Rousseau, we cannot simply choose to return to a natural state, buying some goats and going to live on a commune. Remember, we were driven out of this state by nature itself, by a series of natural accidents. Original nature is no longer there for us.

What we can do, however, is create a society that nurtures and encourages the natural, human qualities, and which reproduces the natural state of freedom, as much as possible. In other words, we must transform society in such a way that within it, humans can be as natural as possible. Rousseau's solution takes three forms or expressions, which are related.

1) THE SOCIAL CONTRACT.

Rousseau refuses Hobbes' idea of a contract between the people that produces an absolute sovereign to whom the individuals must alienate or surrender their freedom. This position he criticizes as it is presented by a Hobbesian political philosopher named Grotius, who uses the example of slavery to show that men can surrender their freedom to a master, just as Hobbes's citizens surrender theirs to the Leviathan. Rousseau, on the other hand, argues that the only reason slaves abandon their freedom is because they are forced to. Freedom is an essential human quality, which cannot be freely given or contracted away. As he writes, "A man who surrenders his freedom is no longer human."

But how can we live in a modern society and remain free, since modern society is a condition where the powerful few have deprived the many of their natural freedom? Rousseau's answer is the concept of the general will. The general will is a community where selfish desires dissolve into the community at large. Through the social contract, as Rousseau defines it, each member does surrender his or her individual rights to the community. However, since the general will is no different from the individual will, this surrender does not translate into a loss or alienation of freedom. The social contract is essentially different from surrendering one's rights to an individual ruler. The law-makers, within a community governed by the social contract, simply follow the dictates of the general will, in drafting legislation. Law is the expression of the general will, of general freedom.

The model for Rousseau's political system was his own city-state of Geneva, where laws were decided by plebiscite, which is why Rousseau says states should be no bigger than cities for them to function properly. This geographical and demographical limitation spares Rousseau, to some extent, from modern-day communitarian or multicultural objections. The restricted, homogeneous nature of Rousseau's political structure is itself based on a notion of community that is far removed from modern states, which necessarily incorporate a multitude of diverse, minority communities and cultures whose general wills may well be distinct from that of other communities or from the nation state as a whole. Nonetheless, Rousseau's social contract is meant to create a human condition that is as natural as possible, as close as possible to the natural condition where individual selfishness, greed, suspicion and conflict did not exist, where the only constraints to freedom were those caused by natural occurrences.

Such a form of government may seem idealistic or communistic to us today. It certainly seems impossible in an age of multiculturalism and community rights. However, in the context of the time, the idea that the individual should only surrender his or her rights to the community of other reasonable individuals, i.e., to the people one belongs to and not to a sovereign ruler, was truly revolutionary. We understand why the American constitution begins with "We the people ..." and why the French Republic was founded on the principles of Liberté, Egalité, Fraternité.

2) EDUCATION.

Rousseau's book *Emile* presents a form of education that is meant to nurture and develop the abused and damaged natural qualities of man. While Rousseau's interest in education may be inspired by his Enlightenment leanings, his pedagogy is a departure from the notion that knowledge, in itself, is liberating. Rather, education should encourage and allow people to rediscover a type of natural innocence and goodness, while still living in society. The idea is also to get away from the traditional educational model of the time, which was based on transmission of knowledge and a hierarchical relationship where the teacher is master and the student is a type of slave.

The student should be encouraged to develop his or her own natural curiosity, free from the domination of the teacher. Above all, education should cultivate and nurture natural feelings, which civilization has suppressed in favor of the stronger passions of jealousy, desire and envy. If you are a recent or somewhat recent graduate from a North American public high school or college, you may recognize in Rousseau the "student-centered" approach you experienced in education: the teacher as guide and facilitator, the encouragement of self-expression, self-esteem, open classrooms etc. Rousseau, along with Socrates (knowledge is within us, questioning brings it out) were likely the principal architects of your educational experience.

3) THE CULTIVATION OF SENTIMENT, OR FEELING.

In the state of nature, the basic human sentiment is one of pity, when faced with the suffering of other humans or animals. Pity is a gentle passion, as is compassion for our fellow living creatures, and should be nurtured through education. Above all, feeling is an inner experience, one through which we come directly in contact with what is natural within us, an idea given full voice in Rousseau's pre-romantic novel *La nouvelle Héloïse*. In fact, through the depth of inner feeling, the human individual communes with nature itself, and may experience the universe as good, true and beautiful. The purest sentiment or feeling is therefore religious, but not in the sense of organized religion. Rather, inner feeling puts us directly in touch with God, who is expressed in nature.

Feeling actually eliminates the religion of priests, another incarnation of authority and enslavement, by making my relationship with God absolutely individual and personal. Feeling eliminates, as Rousseau writes, "the men between God and me."

We see in Rousseau a new definition of the self and its world, one that is very much a part of our contemporary view. Nature is no longer an alien, mechanical configuration, obeying strictly determined physical laws, best expressed in mathematical language. We are neither part of this deterministic mechanism (Hobbes), nor do we stand apart from it, as constantly alienated observers (Descartes). Rather, nature is the source of goodness, truth and beauty, to which we have access through our inner feelings. To the extent that

we subscribe unthinkingly to the belief that "natural" and "good" are virtually synonymous, to the extent that we believe feelings are a source of truth and that nature is essentially good and beautiful, must be protected etc., we are Rousseau's children.

The promotion of individual feeling as a meaningful path to the universality of
nature confers a new, incomparable status on the individual self. The romantic idea, that
the path to truth lies inward, through one's own ability to feel, means that each one of
us holds the key to the highest ideals. One might say this was already true with Socrates
and Plato, where the individual soul was made of finer, more ideal stuff than the worldly
shell that encompassed it, and indeed there is a Platonic echo to be heard in Rousseau.
However, rather than promoting the intellect as the means to these transcendent ends,
Rousseau chooses what is the most natural in all of us, our gentle feelings, as providing
access to this realm. Further, the two thousand intervening years of thought have added
a dimension that was not present in Platonic thought: the idea of inalienable, individual
freedom forming the very foundation of selfhood.

This new and radical view of selfhood as an expression of truth is articulated by
Rousseau in an important, newly conceived literary form: the modern autobiography.
In his posthumously published *Confessions*, Rousseau recounts his life from a deeply personal point of view, hiding nothing, his thoughts, fears, even his perversions. The work is
so detailed, apparently honest and intimate that there appears to be no distance between
the text and the actual life lived. The impact of this brilliant, widely-read work cannot
be underestimated. The absolute equation the *Confessions* establish between art and life
taught a whole generation of Romantics that the best works of art are the heartfelt expressions of one's inner life and truth. The immediate, crucial corollary to this position is that
one's life may itself be construed as a work of art.

We recognize this type of thinking in the contemporary autobiography, where media
and sports stars, criminals, victims, addicts etc., all have important stories to tell. People's
lives are inseparable from their actual productions. We are just as fascinated by the personal lives of our artists, show business personalities, politicians and sports stars as we
are about their actual works. It is not enough to listen to their music, see their films, listen to their speeches, we want to know all about them and their individual, private lives;
if their lives disappoint us, if they don't live up to their art, we condemn them as if they
had made a bad film or written a poor book.

Ultimately, seeing our lives as essentially autobiographical, we accept that everything we do will be judged as the artistic expression of our inner and truest selves. Eating
becomes the "art of dining"; putting clothes on becomes "the art of dressing"; buying
things becomes "the art of shopping"; we present our "selves" on YouTube, Facebook,
etc. Everything we do must say something about who we are, must make a statement.
This is a mixed blessing. While the opportunity to configure our lives as artworks may
add meaning to ourselves and the things we do, it may also be felt as a weighty responsibility. Perhaps some elements of our lives are better left senseless, both for our own sake
and for the sake of art in general!

6. HUME

With Hobbes and Rousseau, we visited what is generally known as political philosophy. Both philosophers are primarily concerned with the question of a just human society. They seek to discover what political conditions are necessary in order for people to live together fairly and peacefully. We have seen how radically different philosophical solutions to human conflict and to the problem of human evils are based on opposed visions of the natural human being.

Scottish philosopher David Hume is also driven by a desire to understand human nature, but his primary concern is scientific, rather than political. Like Descartes, Hume begins by addressing questions of the mind, and particularly its capacity to know the world. Even though, since the story of Adam and Eve, such worldly knowledge has always had moral ramifications, and while Hume is also very interested in moral and political themes, his fundamental interest lies in discovering how and what we can know.

In Descartes, who asked the same question, we saw how the mind itself, the soul or the self, is what can be best known. We saw how knowledge is not drawn directly from the senses, but is the result of clear and distinct thinking. We saw how Descartes construed the world as made up of two separate substances: mind and matter, and how the same dualism is reflected in the human individual, who is made up of mind and body.

David Hume's answer to the problem of knowledge is very different from Descartes's and represents an opposing current of thought: empiricism. I also described Hobbes as an empiricist, and it's no accident both Hobbes and Hume are British. Empiricism is an essentially British, and later, American, way of thinking, and, through the dominance of these cultures, represents the predominant flavor of scientific thought today. Living in an Anglo-American, technological, scientifically-based culture, we tend to be empiricists, or to view the world in an empirical fashion. It is important to understand the roots and limits of this way of thinking because we have largely inherited it. In understanding the relation between the self and the world that empiricism implies, we understand something essential about ourselves.

Empiricism, from the Greek word *empiria* (sensuous experience), holds that knowledge is derived from the senses. It is generally opposed to the current called rationalism, which holds that knowledge is derived from reasoning. Descartes is a model for rationalism because of his belief that knowledge is derived from clear thinking, removed from the experience of the senses. For the purest rationalists, like Descartes, sense experience is flawed and distrusted. It leads us astray. Empiricism, on the contrary, holds that all scientific knowledge must be based on observed, experienced phenomena. Reason alone leads us into unfounded fantasies.

Rationalists generally hold up mathematics as a model for scientific knowledge. This is true for Plato and Descartes and also for the German philosopher, Leibniz, all of them mathematicians, all of them rationalists. Although it may be hard for many recent high school graduates to acknowledge, there is something terribly seductive about mathematical knowledge. In a world of change and uncertainty, mathematics can seem sure, universal and even eternal. Statements are either true or false. 5 + 7 equals 12, necessarily and forever, or so it seems. This is because mathematics, like certain logical forms, works on deduction. Statements follow necessarily from other statements. There is no need to verify them with experiment. From what I know about arithmetic, I can deduce that adding 1 to an odd number will always give me an even number, without actually carrying out an experiment using apples or stones or blades of grass.

Empiricists, on the other hand, generally hold up physics, or natural science, as a model of knowledge. Copernicus's theory of a heliocentric cosmos was a better theory than the opposing one because observation (e.g., by Galileo) backed it up. Laws of physics, even the most mathematically abstract ones, are only substantiated when they are supported by experiment and observation. In its purest form, empiricism tends to rely on inductive, rather than deductive logic. We gather together a certain number of individual, observed phenomena, or facts, and make a general conclusion. In its purest form, rationalism claims to deduce true statements, without any sensory interference.

In their purest forms, however, both rationalism and empiricism encounter difficulties and contradictions. Rationalism has difficulty coming up with new knowledge about the world. Without relying on sense data, it cannot know anything concretely real. On the other hand, empiricism has difficulty attaining the degree of certainty that can be attained through deduction. Operating principally through induction, i.e., by generalizing a conclusion from a number of individual facts or cases, empiricism is always in danger of running into a counter example, the best it can arrive at is likelihood. It is particularly challenged by such traditional objects of metaphysics as the True, the Good, the Beautiful, the soul or God, which, by definition, lie beyond sensory knowledge and cannot be arrived at by induction. Thus, the rationalist Descartes concludes he can know the soul (mind) better than he can know the world. While for the empirical Hobbes, the mind loses much of its particular status. It is simply part of the observed world.

Having acquired a great deal from his predecessor, John Locke, Hume's empiricism is more sophisticated than that of Hobbes. Yet as an empiricist, Hume also encounters insurmountable difficulties when he comes to consider the nature of the mind as conscious self-identity. This is the theme that I want to explore: If knowledge must be based on sensuous experience, how can the self become an object of knowledge? How do I experience myself empirically as "a thing that thinks," to use Descartes's definition of the self? This question takes Hume, and us, to the limits of knowledge and hence, to the philosophical problem of skepticism.

A contemporary of Rousseau's, David Hume was born in Edinburgh, in 1711, four years after the incorporation of Scotland into the United Kingdom. His father died when he was three years old and, like Hobbes, he was brought up by an uncle, in Hume's case, a clergyman.

At the age of eleven, he entered Edinburgh College where he studied logic, mathematics and Newtonian physics. He read Descartes, the Cartesian philosopher Malebranche, and also the ancient and modern poets. His education was markedly different from that of Descartes, born just over a century earlier; the only predominantly Aristotelian element in Hume's studies was in the area of logic. Although he was supposed to study law, Hume, following the honored philosophical tradition, refused to pursue that profession. Instead, he traveled to France where he resided at the college of La Flèche, where Descartes had studied. Here, Hume wrote his masterpiece, *Treatise on Human Nature*, in 1734. The book had little success.

In 1741, he wrote his *Moral and Political Essays*. The essay style suited him well (he had read Montaigne, inventor of the modern essay form) and the book was widely read. He almost got a university position in Glasgow but for better or for worse, Hume does not become the first university professor to figure in our story of philosophy. Instead, he becomes a diplomat and accompanies another uncle, the General Saint-Clair, to Vienna and Turin.

In 1748, at the age of 37, he published his famous *Inquiry Concerning Human Understanding*, a substantial re-working of the first part of his great *Treatise*. He followed this work with his *Political Discourses*, and his *Inquiry Concerning the Principles of Morals* (1751). Hume also wrote a four volume history of England, which became a bestseller, and other works on religion, the passions (emotions), and art. In the 1760s, as a diplomat in Paris, Hume became very popular at various literary salons, and with the *Philosophes*. He befriended the banished Rousseau and even put him up for a time, until the two fell out, probably due to the latter's difficult personality. Returning to England, he attained the position of government undersecretary, before retiring to Edinburgh, the center of what is known as the Scottish Enlightenment, which included such luminaries as Adam Smith, James Steuart and Adam Ferguson. Home again, in this Athens of the north, Hume died in 1776, the year of the American Revolution.

In writing about a philosopher whose life and oeuvre were so full and rich, it may seem odd that I choose to concentrate this brief chapter on what might be construed as his failure, on his unsuccessful attempt to know himself empirically. However, if each philosophy in this story did not have its limits, one chapter would not lead to another and we would not have a story! A great philosopher is one who pushes the limits as far as is humanly possible and then is honest enough to acknowledge them. Hume's philosophy is great because of its Socratic reluctance to settle for any convenient answers, the constant restlessness of its reflections, and the tangible insights it offers us in our understanding of ourselves. Part of that understanding involves the honest recognition of our limits, the fact that we will never know everything, but that beyond those limits, or in spite of them, there is still human life, in all its wonderful complexity.

Like Descartes, Hume believes that before we can really know anything, we must get to know the thing that knows. We must answer the question, "how can we know?" as a foundation to science. In other words, human nature, as a knowing self or subject, must become the object of our investigation. The human, knowing subject is at the center of the sciences. As Hume puts it, "All the sciences have a relation, either greater or lesser, with human nature." Therefore, we have to know the thing that knows before we can know the world. Scientific truth is relative to the knowing human mind.

The interest in human nature as a condition for science and truth is a modern idea, appearing with Descartes. For Plato, the truth is there. It is ultimately found in the realm of Ideas, whether we come to know it or not. For Aristotle, as well, the truth of things is their essence, although essence is presented in the things' worldly forms. The modern idea involves the quest to discover human nature because scientific truth is dependent upon it. Hence, in the field of political philosophy, with Hobbes and Rousseau for example, knowing human nature is a condition for learning how humans can be good, and live together in society.

Consequently, we can now say that the existence of the True and the Good is dependent upon us and our ability to know them. This is a huge departure from the Greco-Christian belief that the True and the Good (and the Beautiful) are self-subsistent substances of which we, poor humans, must make ourselves worthy. Now, the True and the Good (and the Beautiful) are only there for us, through our abilities to know, to will and to create or judge art. Bringing the three greatest objects of knowledge closer to home, however, presents us with perhaps the greatest challenge of all. Now we must obey the onerous injunction of the Oracle, "know thyself!"

For Hume, as for Descartes, discovering essential human nature means knowing how we know things. Also like Descartes, Hume looks for the simplest, most fundamental elements from which he seeks to deduce his theory of knowledge. Rather than beginning, as we saw in Descartes, with a reductive skepticism, stripping away all uncertainty in order to arrive at one sure thing, Hume begins with knowledge as we actually experience it. His approach is much more down to earth, more Scottish, we might say. Rather than shutting ourselves in a darkened room, as Frenchman René Descartes had done, and embarking on the contemplative madness of radical doubt, let's look at the real, living experience of knowing, as we actually carry it out. What are we conscious of when we think? What do we actually feel when we think?

In fact, says Hume, we feel two sorts of things: impressions and ideas. Impressions are sensations, passions, emotions that strike us immediately, through our outer senses and our inner feelings. On the other hand, ideas are reflected images (*eidos* = Greek for image) of these impressions.

It is important to understand that the impressions come first. The ideas are copies of impressions, whether the impressions are sense perceptions or emotions. Simple or single ideas are always the corresponding copies of simple impressions. I can have an idea of what pineapple tastes like, because I have already had the simple impression of tasting it. I can have an idea of red, because I have already seen it, as an impression on my sight. I can have an idea of anger, because I have already felt it. The idea cannot inversely produce an impression. I cannot derive the impression of the taste of pineapple from the idea, if I have never tasted it. This is why Hume comes up with his startling claim, in his essay on the passions, that "reason is and must always be the slave of the passions." Our ideas are always derived from our sensory or emotional impressions.

Undeniably, we experience complex ideas and our thinking is more than a series of unrelated copies of our immediate impressions. Where do complex ideas come from? How can we explain what Hobbes had referred to as "trains of thought" in a more satisfying, less mechanical way?

First, complex ideas are not copies of corresponding complex impressions. Although we can have complex impressions, things that strike us in a simultaneous or ambiguous way, these are not translated directly into complex ideas. Ideas are combined by reason or that part of it called the imagination. Thus, I can have the complex idea of a golden calf, even if I have never seen one. My imagination combines two different impressions, "calf" and "golden" together to create the mythical idea of a golden calf. However, for a complex idea to be of scientific value, it must combine its simple ideas, which correspond to simple impressions, according to certain rules or principles. This is the basis of Hume's empiricism.

Regarding the science of nature, our impressions are derived from the senses and our ideas are copies of our impressions. Our ideas are connected together through the imagination and this is what reasoning does. The imagination must be understood in a different way than it is today. In this pre-romantic world, it is not to be thought of as creative fantasy, but rather simply as the faculty that connects ideas. It does so according to a number of principles including resemblance, contiguity, and cause and effect. These three main principles of the imagination are to ideas what Newton's law of gravitation is to physics: they express the laws of a force of attraction that is inherent in ideas themselves, just as Newton's law expresses a force within objects themselves.

Our imagination may connect ideas because they resemble one another. For example, I observe many impressions of green (fields, clothes, leaves, grass, eyes), each of which is copied as a simple idea. Since the ideas all resemble each other, my imagination produces the general idea of green. Or, according to the second principle, because I have ideas of contiguous impressions, of impressions that seem to physically run together, my imagination brings together the separate ideas into one "thing." For example, a tree is a complex idea formed from the contiguous ideas of trunk, branches, leaves etc. Or again, because one impression and its idea always seem to occur just before another impression and its idea, I imagine that the first idea is causing the second. I imagine the complex idea of cause and effect.

The point about cause and effect is particularly important, because it revolutionizes the way philosophers and scientists view causation, and along with it, the world, reason and truth. For what does it mean to understand the reasons for worldly things, to discover their truth, if not to know their causes, what has caused them? This was certainly Aristotle's view, and it largely determined how Western thought regarded causation, reason and reality for two thousand years. According to this view, the laws of cause and effect are anchored in nature itself, defining the very soul, not only of worldly things but ultimately of God himself, the unmoved mover, the first and final cause of everything.

Hume is saying that the law of causation, as the necessary relation between cause and effect, is nowhere but in the human mind, existing only as a basic principle of the imagination. If we understand things as being caused or causing, it is simply through habit, because our imagination has come to see the ideas of correlated events, where one always follows the other, in terms of cause and effect. However, there is nothing in the objects themselves that necessarily implies they are the effects or the causes of other things.

I can shoot a billiard ball at another one and say the first ball will cause the other ball to move when it is hit. But, in fact, there is nothing in the action between the billiard balls that contains this relation. The cue ball could actually rebound from the other ball, or it might go right through it or, as always happens in my experience, the movement of one ball may indeed be transferred to another. It is only because I have seen the same thing or similar things happen countless times, that I imagine, through habit, that the first ball will necessarily cause the other ball to move. In Hume's terms, the idea of causality, as a necessary connection or law of nature, has no corresponding impression. It is a complex idea, arrived at through the imagination. The idea of cause is a product of a principle of our imagination, a way of joining together two ideas that often succeed one another.

All one can really say is that events that seem to follow one another are correlated. Although we are still, in our daily dealings, in our intuitive understanding of the world and in our language, still children of Aristotle, much of modern science follows Hume and looks at causation as a matter of pure correlation. There is no *necessary* causal link. Events occur with a measurable frequency when other events are present. Natural causation is a superfluous concept, replaced by predictability and probability. This is even true of the supposed laws of nature. As Hume remarks, just because the sun has risen every day for the past ten thousand years, there's no certainty it will rise tomorrow.

In fact, such a statement highlights the problem of any empirical knowledge, of establishing knowledge inductively arrived at through observed facts. The conclusion is always a generalization involving an inference that is a leap of faith. Nothing arrived at inductively is ever absolutely certain; it always reflects a degree of probability. We can never conclude there is causal necessity in nature. This is a very modern thought. The supposed laws of nature, like cause and effect, are in fact human laws that we impose on nature. They are the product of human minds and belief.

Rational thought or inquiry reveals this truth: that science rests on degrees of probability and belief rather than on absolute certainty. Rational inquiry therefore leads to a position of relative skepticism, where the things we thought most certain are now only probable. This includes uncertainty regarding the existence of the outer world, or nature, itself. If all that I know is derived from subjective impressions and the ideas which are the mental copies of those impressions, connected according to my imagination, how can I know what is beyond those impressions? For Hume, even the existence of the outside world is a matter of belief, of strong probability.

The skepticism we encounter in Hume is unlike Descartes's, who employs it as part of a scientific method aimed at finding the one certainty from which other truths could be deduced. We might say that Descartes's skepticism is a preliminary to seeking truth, whereas Hume's skepticism comes at the end and limits the truths we have found. Descartes's skepticism comes just before dawn; Hume's rises like mist after dusk.

It is perhaps ironic that a figure of the Scottish Enlightenment should conclude that we cannot know things absolutely, that we can only believe them to be true, to a greater or lesser degree, or we can suspend our judgment. Certainly, we can suspend our judgment with regard to knowing the existence of God, or the reality of human freedom, or the soul, or the reality of the world. Or we can believe them, simply because it is practical to do so. Hume makes this distinction between the philosophical sphere of thought, which is not only difficult but leads us to doubt those things which appear the most certain, and the sphere of common life and concerns where we act as if the world is knowable. This is part of his tremendous appeal as a thinker: he was very much part of everyday life and enjoyed its comforts and entertainments. In a way, he is a reluctant philosopher, conscious of the ease of ordinary life, and the labor, pain and bitter fruits offered by philosophical thought. Like all great philosophers, however, he is driven to think about things.

Hume's restless inquiry and skepticism, along with his reluctance towards philosophy, are clearly expressed in those writings, from his first *Treatise*, where he attempts to know human identity, the essence of the self or consciousness.

We saw how Descartes arrives at his knowledge of the self, or the soul, through a process of skepticism that eliminated all uncertain knowledge and arrived at one intuitive certainty. I think therefore I am. This certainty is "a priori," a Latin term meaning prior to any sensory experience and thus dependent on reasoning alone. Descartes's famous conclusion, is actually inferred from a deductive argument, a categorical syllogism, with a hidden premise.

Everything that thinks, exists.

I think.

Therefore, I exist.

According to his own principles, Hume must know the self empirically, or "a posteriori," through what he calls sensuous impressions, because that's where all knowledge is derived from. The self Hume seeks to know is the Cartesian self, i.e., the self as a self-identical and simple substance, that which makes me who I am and not another, and keeps me that way over time. I certainly seem to have a simple idea of this self that I am. However, the problem, for Hume, is that there is no corresponding simple impression on which this idea of self is based. Instead, we have an infinite number of impressions and ideas that constantly impress themselves on the body and then cross the mind, like actors on a stage. People are "a bundle or collection of different perceptions, which succeed each other with an inconceivable rapidity and are in constant flux and movement."

There is no identity and no simplicity to the impressions I experience, so why do I have this propensity to ascribe an identity to these different perceptions, understand them as "me"? The answer must be that the imagination, which works according to the gathering principles of resemblance, contiguity, and cause and effect, creates the fiction of identity out of the multiplicity of ideas stemming from the sensuous impressions.

In other words, because our impressions are copied by ideas that resemble each other, which are contiguous (joined) to each other or seem to be related to one another through causation, our imaginations create the fiction of an identity.

To demonstrate, Hume uses the example of "any mass of matter," in other words, an object outside his body. The demonstration is similar to Descartes's taking the piece of wax as an example, although Descartes uses the wax to show what he can know of the outer world through the senses (nothing), whereas Hume uses the "mass of matter" to show what we can know about ourselves (nothing, as we will see).

Hume notes that although we may add a small, additional piece of matter to the object, like modeling clay, we still assume the object is identical, even though this is not actually true. The same applies to objects that change gradually, like a plant or an animal body. The change implies that the object is no longer self-identical, and yet because the change is gradual and the states are similar, our imaginations ascribe identity to the object. However, this is a fiction of the imagination. Hume now applies this analysis to personal identity, postulating that "the identity which we ascribe to the mind of man is only a fictitious one, and of a like kind with that which we ascribe to objects."

To show this, Hume explains identity, this time personal identity, in terms of resemblance and causation (the imagination). Drawing on the work of his famous predecessor John Locke, Hume postulates that in the mind, resemblance and causation are related to memory. It is because we "raise up the images of past perceptions" and because those images (ideas) resemble the perceptions, that we have memory. This makes the mind appear to have continuity, which we take for personal identity. The same is true of causation. Memory enables us to link together ideas as if one caused the other, and this also gives us an impression of continuity, of self-identity.

However, having put forward this hypothesis, Hume's relentless sense of inquiry and intellectual honesty causes him to then show how memory cannot really establish self-identity. In fact, most of our past ideas and impressions are forgotten. Our past is far from continuous; it is filled with great holes and gaps, and yet we still have a feeling of identity. Memory therefore does not produce self-identity. The preliminary conclusion is a skeptical one: "that all the nice and subtle questions concerning personal identity can never possibly be decided."

What we do know is that the idea of personal identity, since it relies on principles of the imagination, is a fiction. Perhaps such questions should not even concern us philosophically but should be regarded as "grammatical rather than philosophical difficulties." Perhaps it is because our language causes us to use the first person singular "I" that we assume this thing actually exists when, in fact, I am simply a figment of my imagination. Hume thus initiates an important tendency in modern philosophy (whether Anglo-American or Continental) which affirms that most traditional metaphysical questions (God, freedom, the soul) arise from our ambiguous use of common language and its grammatical structures. We can eliminate many problems or at least approach them in a different way by reinventing philosophical discourse.

The passage at the end of the *Treatise*, is a wonderful depiction of the skeptical dilemma that Hume encounters in his inquiry. He admits he cannot answer the big philosophical questions. Ultimately, I cannot know the answers to such questions as "Where am I, or what? From what causes do I derive my existence and to what condition shall I return? What beings surround me? Etc." These must remain objects of belief, or conjecture. Thus, Hume finds himself in "the deepest darkness" of skeptical doubt, "the most deplorable condition imaginable," analogous to Descartes's condition at the end of his first Meditation, when he has evacuated all he has known. In Hume's case, however, it is not the discovery of his selfhood that saves him from this condition. Rather, it is real life itself that saves him from skeptical depression. He is drawn back into the everyday world where, as he puts it, "I dine, I play a game of backgammon, I converse and am merry with my friends."

For a true philosopher like Hume, this state of blissful oblivion cannot last. As we see in the appendix to his discussion, Hume cannot help but return, almost obsessively, to his inquiry into personal identity. Here, he briefly summarizes his argument that personal identity is a fiction: we are really a bundle of perceptions forged together by the imagination. But then he himself admits that his reasoning has been defective. After all, what is this "principle of connection which binds the perceptions together" if not some sort of personal identity of thought? There must be something there that connects all "my" impressions together and makes them "mine." What is that thing that creates the fiction of me, if not *me*? Perhaps it is thought reflecting on itself that creates identity. Personal identity is perhaps self-reflection, and yet this still fails to explain those principles that "unite our successive perceptions in our thought or consciousness." Finally, once again, the answer is to "plead the privilege of the skeptic," to perhaps have a glass of wine and another game of backgammon!

  Immanuel Kant will take up the skeptical challenge. His response will involve an attempt to show that the self, as we can know it, is fundamentally the very action of synthesizing that Hume designated as the principles of the imagination. I am that which brings together in such a way as to form *my* experience. I synthesize, therefore I am.

7. KANT

The German philosopher, Immanuel Kant, read and admired Hume, claiming the latter had woken him from his "dogmatic slumber" by introducing him to new ways of looking at the things he had taken for granted. Kant accepted Hume's discovery that the mind receives sensuous impressions and that these are different from the thoughts or representations that Hume called ideas. As well, Kant agreed that there must be some internal principles that forge these impressions into mental representations, and that, as Hume seemed to imply, these principles of the imagination were somehow related to personal identity. He could not, however, accept Hume's skepticism regarding knowledge of the self, the world and God.

Although Hume had said that, as selves, we are only bundles of perceptions, he does admit that there is something that connects these individual perceptions together to form personal conscious thought. Kant comes up with the revolutionary idea that it is the action of synthesis, of bringing together the images of our experience, which actually constitutes the self.

By accepting Hume's premise that the mind only knows impressions of the outside world, or objectivity, Kant also accepts the fact that we cannot know the things themselves that lie behind our impressions. This was another source of Hume's skepticism, the fact that I can never be absolutely sure of the existence of a real world beyond my senses. However, for Kant, the fact we can never know the things in themselves beyond our sense impressions is again not a source of skepticism. It simply defines what knowledge humans are capable of. All I can know comes from my impressions, but perhaps this leaves room for another way of apprehending the world.

If the world comes to me through an infinite diversity of sense impressions, how can I make sense of it? And what is this self, this "I" that does make sense of the world? We tend to believe, naïvely, that the world simply is, that what we see is what is there.

But consider it carefully. As a body and sense organs, all you are really receiving is a multitude of impressions. The world presents itself as a jumble of raw sense data. Imagine a world where all life has been destroyed, and yet where all the security video cameras continue to function. With no one to ever look at the images, to understand them and make sense of them, what would those images represent? They would be pure, meaningless data, varying shades of light and dark. As well, the "self" receiving such data is no more than an empty mechanism of lenses and magnetic tape. Truly, the way we perceive the world says much about who we are, and vice versa.

If the world first presents itself to our senses as unprocessed, meaningless data, then who am I that takes this material and makes sense of it, and how do I do it? How do I come to perceive meaningful objects and not just raw impulses? And more importantly, how do I come to understand them and make knowledge statements about them? Further, if all I can know is a result of sense impressions, how do I even know the actual world exists? Or that my representations are faithful ones?

Immanuel Kant was born in Königsberg, Prussia, in 1724. Although he was to become celebrated all over Europe, he spent his whole life in that small town and died there in 1804. He came from a modest background, as Rousseau had. Kant's parents wanted him to become a pastor, and sent him to school where he learned Latin and mathematics. He enrolled at the University of Königsberg in 1740, where he studied Newtonian physics and philosophy, both classical and post-Cartesian.

Unfortunately, Kant was so poor that he was forced to interrupt his studies and work as a private tutor for the wealthy, a common destiny for impecunious, young scholars at the time. He taught his young charges everything from logic to geography. In 1762, he read Rousseau's *Emile*, which, as he writes, taught him "to respect men" for something other than their knowledge. He also read David Hume, and was particularly taken by his critique of causation. During this period, Kant wrote prolifically on many subjects, physics, astronomy, anthropology, morals, mental health ... Finally, in 1770, when he was 46 years old, he defended his doctoral thesis and was able to teach at the University, the same one he had attended thirty years earlier.

After eleven years of work, in 1781, he published his first major book, the first of his three famous Critiques, the *Critique of Pure Reason*. He was now 57 years old. A reworked, better known, second edition appeared in 1787. His *Critique of Practical Reason* appeared in 1788, and two years later, his third great work was published, the *Critique of Judgment*. These three major works deal with what Kant sees as three fundamental human questions: What can I know? What must I believe? What may I hope for? Similarly, we can say Kant's Critiques deal with scientific knowing (truth), ethics/freedom (the good), and art/nature (the beautiful). In other words still, they deal with the main objects of metaphysical thought: the soul (what can it know?), the world (am I free or determined?), and God (is there divine/natural providence?).

These traditional objects of metaphysical reflection, however, are approached in a new way—a critical way—which has become one of the principal forms philosophy has taken since Kant. His three critiques also make Kant perhaps the most important philosopher since Aristotle. Why do I say this? Because it is impossible, today, to discuss questions of knowledge, ethics, or esthetics, in an informed way, without referring to Kant.

Critical philosophy, as Kant practices it, is one that examines itself, and particularly its own foundations. The word "criticize" comes from the Greek word *krinein*, which means to discern. For Kant, criticizing means analyzing, understanding and discerning the limits of our ability to make knowledge claims, moral claims and esthetic claims. In general terms, it means making an object of study that which has already been presented. This has given rise to such philosophical movements as "theory of knowledge"or epistemology, logical positivism, social theory, hermeneutics, deconstruction, all forms of philosophy that tend to analyze what is there rather than speculate on what might be, although it is hard to do one without the other. The critical tradition also underlies the way philosophy is generally practiced today at the university: our objects of study are often the philosophies that have been, language that is used, science that is practiced, etc. Perhaps it is no accident that Kant is the first specimen we encounter, in our story, of a species of philosopher that has now become predominant: the university professor. It is also perhaps no accident that the first university professor we meet should be German, for it is in 19th-Century Germany that the first modern, state-supported (i.e., secular, republican) universities were born.

Kant spent his whole life studying and teaching at Königsberg, and was happy to do so. In any case, he believed in habit and regularity, feeling it prolonged life and enabled one to produce more work. (He was probably right!) He lived as a bachelor because he felt marriage took up too much time and effort, keeping one servant who woke him up at the same time every morning, leaving a cup of coffee and one pipe of tobacco waiting on his breakfast table. Kant was perhaps the first to write on modern dietary notions, affirming that one could influence one's health by following rational, thought-out regimens. He worked in the morning, had long, copious lunches with groups of friends and much stimulating conversation. He read in the afternoon, and took a long walk in the evening, the same number of steps each time. He died following one of his walks, in 1804.

Kant is a prime representative of what is known as the German Enlightenment, the *Aufklärung*. The later German version of the movement shares with its French counterpart a belief in Reason as the accomplishment of human destiny, and perfecting. He also shares with the French *Lumières* the belief that reason liberates us or frees us from the bonds of superstition, demagogic religion and dogmatic learning. This is what Kant means when he, the philosophy professor, writes that philosophy cannot be taught, only philosophizing can. In other words, the goal of philosophy is to make students "think for themselves." Reason, in this sense, is liberating. It does not consist of amassing knowledge, but in learning how to think. To know how to think, students must have clear notions of the concepts they use. In this way, philosophy is critical, i.e., discerning (*krinein*), of definitions, of limits of reasoning.

The liberating aspect of Reason has necessarily moral/ethical ramifications. For only as free, self-determining agents do we encounter moral concerns, where we can (and must) decide what is right or wrong. If we're not free, there is no moral problem. We simply do what we have to.

Kant's famous question, "What can I know?" implies the limits of reasoning. His two other crucial questions (What must I believe? What may I hope for?) imply there is something of interest that lies beyond reasoning, something more than the dark emptiness of skeptical doubt. Kant had read and appreciated Rousseau, and therefore acknowledged that feeling and sentiment were an essential part of being human, something that puts the individual in touch with Godliness. More precisely, beyond reasonable knowledge, there is room for inner feeling in the form of Kantian faith or belief. By establishing the limits of reason, we also establish the area of faith and belief.

The religious dimension is an aspect that distinguishes much of the German *Aufklärung* from the French *Lumières*. Reason does not necessarily exclude faith in God. In fact, faith and reasoning must collaborate as two elements of knowing the same universal object, through something called Reason (with a capital 'R'). Such a collaboration cannot help but lead to a radical reinterpretation of how we look at both faith and reasoning, as well as how we understand knowledge. Indeed, the subsequent philosophical period, known as German Idealism (e.g., Hegel), will seek to initiate and even carry out this new form of (absolute) knowing, through Reason (with a capital 'R').

The project of the *Critique of Pure Reason* is to establish the limits of reasoning in order to secure the domain of faith. Pure reason refers to the traditional forms of metaphysical argument that we encountered in Plato and Descartes. Such forms are entirely rational or "a priori" and aimed at knowing the traditional objects of metaphysics: God, the soul, freedom (or the possibility of freedom in the world). These objects are obviously beyond sensory (a posteriori) knowledge. I cannot directly know God, the soul or freedom through my senses, which can only give me individual impressions of individual worldly things.

The problem is that this type of pure metaphysical reasoning has given us nothing certain. Each metaphysician has come up with his particular theories on the self, the nature of human freedom or God. Can I prove God exists? If so, how? Does this proof hold or is it a circular argument? What about freedom? Are humans free or are they determined by natural causation, by chains of events that even determine the illusion of our freedom? As for the human soul, is it simple and unique or part of a larger, universal substance? Is it immortal or mortal? Is it essentially mine or do I just borrow it while I live? And who am I? The fact that such questions are still debated seems to indicate the failure of metaphysical knowledge, of pure reasoning. The *Critique of Pure Reason* is a critique of metaphysics, or an attempt to find its limits.

Traditionally, claims the *Critique*, knowledge involves two types of reasoning. The first type is purely a priori. It is ideally confined to mathematics and logic, sciences that are non-empirical, or independent of sensory knowledge. I may apply mathematics and logic to apples, oranges, bridges or motors, but I don't have to. The purely rational sciences of mathematics and logic are traditionally considered analytic, rather than synthetic. This means that from the analysis of a set of basic principles or axioms, conclusions are drawn or inferred. Euclid's axioms of geometry are a good example of the analytical process. The conclusions drawn from the original principles actually contain nothing new. They are found out as a result of analyzing, or breaking down, the initial principles, and then analyzing the new principles and so on until a whole system appears. Each subsequent principle is broken down or analyzed to find new principles.

This process can also be described as deduction. From the axiom, all triangles have three angles that add up to 180 degrees, I can deduce, by analyzing the principle, another principle: if one of the angles is 90 degrees, the other two must add up to 90 degrees. However, the second principle is actually contained in the first one; no new knowledge is acquired which is not already contained in the original axiom on the triangle.

The other type of reasoning is "a posteriori" or empirical. It is traditionally considered to be synthetic rather than analytic. Different facts or intuitions are synthesized together to produce new knowledge. It can also be described as inductive, rather than deductive. This type of reasoning is used in natural, experimental sciences. I observe a number of cases, e.g., where water freezes at different temperatures at different altitudes, and conclude or generalize that atmospheric pressure affects the freezing point of water. My conclusion is a statement of new knowledge, which I didn't possess before and which is the result of my empirical observations.

Kant's original intuition was to say that the distinction between "a priori" reasoning as entirely analytical and empirical reasoning as synthetic is not correct. There are, he maintained, a priori (non-empirical) judgments that are also synthetic. Mathematics, he claimed, can be both a priori and synthetic. His famous example is simply the addition of two numbers.

Take $5 + 7 = 12$.

According to Kant, the result, 12, is not contained in the first part of the equation. The concept of 12 represents something new. In other words, no amount of analysis of the numbers 5 and 7 will give us the new number, the new concept of 12.

Mathematics represents a model for true knowledge, or science, for Kant, as it has for many philosophers. Mathematics seems to provide us with knowledge that is absolute, universal and certain. Surely this is something to aspire to. The problem is that philosophy has been flailing around for centuries, without ever establishing anything like mathematical certainty. This is strange, since metaphysical philosophy claims to operate like mathematics, by using pure reason to produce new knowledge. In other words, metaphysics claims to make synthetic, a priori judgments, just like mathematics does. So why hasn't pure philosophical reasoning attained any certain knowledge, anything as clear and true as $5 + 7 = 12$?

Indeed, when metaphysics reasons on such philosophical subjects as the existence of God, the nature of the human soul or the possibility of freedom in the natural universe, it achieves only conflict, disputation and uncertainty. By examining how synthetic a priori judgments are possible, Kant hopes to discern (*krinein* = critique) how far they may be used. In this way Kant's critique of pure reason is a critique of synthetic a priori judgments and, above all, a critique of metaphysical reasoning. In other words, what happens when we attempt to know objects other than mathematical objects, objects that are supposed to have objective reality, objects like God, the world and the soul, and yet which are not immediately present to the senses? To begin with, we must understand human understanding, the faculty which enables us to know the things of the world. Like Hume, Kant asks the question, how do we actually come to know things in general?

The first structures, the foundation of our understanding, are what Kant calls the pure forms of sensuous intuition (feeling), time and space. Kant refers to this idea as his Copernican revolution, akin to Copernicus's revolutionary insight that the sun was at the centre of the cosmos, not the earth. Rather than considering time and space as existing in outer objectivity, in nature, Kant maintains that they are subjective conditions of experience. Time and space are the primary conditions of our perceiving reality generally. The fact that we can experience the world is only possible because we have this general intuition (or feeling) within ourselves, of time and space, particularly time. These internal, intimate intuitions allow us to simply be here and now with regard to the world. They are at the foundation of our feeling of selfhood and our apprehension of the world.

Everything we experience is given in time, otherwise we would have no personal experience of the succession of the infinite variety of sense data that we are constantly bombarded with. Without our internal sense of time, we would have no feeling of change, or motion, or becoming. The intuition of time is at the core of our being as selves. Through it, we feel ourselves as being situated, at the center of a here and now. Outside this subjective framework, where time is an internal condition for sensuous intuition or feeling, time is nothing. The universe does not operate on laws of temporal ordering. We order the universe temporally.

For Kant, the manifold sensations of the world that come to us through the senses and are experienced as being in space and time must be synthesized as objects, or rather, as representations of objects. This first power of synthesis or organization is the imagination, a power that exists a priori in the mind. It is a "blind but indispensable function of the soul." The imagination is the faculty that produces unified images or representations from the manifold sense data, just as Hume's principles of the imagination synthesized sense impressions into ideas. As with Hume, Kant's imagination does not work according to fancy or fantasy. It is a power that first unifies the diverse sense data into objects, thus allowing us to understand these objects according to certain categories.

This type of understanding no longer takes place at the level of sensibility, of the pure forms of intuition. We are now dealing with rational thought itself. Human understanding takes the materials it is supplied with, the representations or objects that have been forged by the imagination from the sense data, and further synthesizes this material under mental categories, which Kant describes as a priori concepts. It is this stage of synthesis that produces knowledge.

For Kant, to know is to make judgments or statements that assign a predicate to a grammatical subject. He uses the example "Every metal is a body." We might also add such simple statements as "iron is a metal," "the earth is a planet," "the moon is about ¼ the size of the earth," etc. The categories of understanding are also the grammatical categories under which we make these judgments, or statements of predication. Such knowledge judgments or statements are divided into four categories: Quantity, Quality, Modality and Relation. In other words, when I make a knowledge statement about something, I attach a predicate to it in such a way as to say something about its quantity (e.g., it is one, two, many, big, smaller, etc.), its quality (e.g., it is a metal, light, a gas, a force etc.), its modality (e.g., it is necessary, possible, real, inexistent, etc.), or its relation (e.g., it is caused by something, an effect of something, only occurs when something else occurs, etc.). Whenever we understand an object, we judge or make statements about it according to at least one of these categories of judgments.

This means that for us to understand any given object, it must first fall under one of the categories. The categories are preconditions to our understanding reality. They are a priori concepts, in that they determine what empirical data we may apprehend. And yet, something is missing. For knowledge to happen, it is not enough for objects to be objects of thought in an abstract way. They must be objects of *my* thought, otherwise, my understanding would simply be filled with foreign, miscellaneous objects and judgments. A condition of knowledge is that *I hold* it to be true. The fundamental unifying force that "accompanies all my representations" says Kant, is the "I think," in other words the Cartesian "cogito." Kant calls this power "the synthetic unity of apperception." It is what makes our understanding subjective and knowledge personal.

Because knowledge statements are always attached to individual understanding, this does not mean, however, that they are subjective in an arbitrary or relativistic way. The categories of understanding are derived from the traditional forms of logic, and since all rational (human) beings are capable of logical thought, they must share the same categories of understanding. The universality of the categories of understanding means that knowledge has the ability to be objectively shared, beyond my own individual judgments. As knowledge, my judgments are always capable of being communicated, taught, discussed, challenged, proven, etc., because, as rational beings, our discussions always involve questions of quantity, quality, modality and relation.

The forms of our understanding, i.e., time, space and the categories, are the conditions of subjective experience, through which we may make sense of, and know, the world. Conversely, these forms are meaningless without the sense data supplied from the outer world. They need the sense data in order to make sense! My subjective forms of understanding are nothing without the world to give them content. This is very different from the pure Cartesian self, the pure "I think," which existed as a distinct substance, separate and independent from the world. In Kant, we have the beginnings of the idea that consciousness, or the self, only exists as consciousness *of* something other than itself, a notion that will be given full expression in Hegel.

What about the limits of pure reason, the question Kant begins with? We now see that the understanding mind can only know objects that occur to it through the senses. The understanding must have sense data in order to make knowledge, in order to make judgments according to its categories. So we can conclude, according to Kant, that knowledge of the understanding is empirical. This means that objects like God, the soul, the universe are beyond our knowledge because they simply do not fit into the categories of our understanding. We may believe we witness the effects of God, feelings of the soul or elements of the universe, but these objects themselves are purely metaphysical, beyond the physical, not fully given to us in time and space. They cannot be the objects of our understanding and so, in this sense, metaphysical knowledge is impossible. Pure metaphysical reasoning, beyond the senses and the understanding, can never arrive at knowledge.

This appears to be a skeptical conclusion similar to Hume's. However, for Kant, the limits of scientific knowledge are far from being an entirely negative discovery. In fact, the limits of knowledge define the space of my freedom and the possibility I have of being a moral being. Far from being useless, pure reason guarantees the possibility I have of determining my actions in a way that is free from the interference of natural causes and desires. How is this possible?

Briefly, because the categories of my understanding, and of knowledge, are always dependent upon how outer nature (i.e., the world) affects me through my senses, and because pure reason is beyond the categories, pure reason may be free from natural influence and determination. This means that to the extent I can let reason alone determine my will, my will becomes entirely free of interference from outer causes and motivations. When I am determined solely by pure reason, then I do not will things because of such worldly, natural determinations as hunger, sexual desire, power over others, my genetic makeup, my unfortunate upbringing, etc. I will things because my reason tells me it is right and good to do so. Reason is inherently disobedient, even rebellious. It does not obey the laws of nature; it makes laws that determine the free will. The limits of my understanding therefore define the space of my freedom and without freedom, as I mentioned above, there is no possibility of morality. Pure reason thus ensures the freedom of our wills and enables us to be moral beings. But here, Reason should be written with a capital "R."

Finally, with his idea of Reason, Kant introduces a new form of discourse into philosophy. Since it cannot make the type of knowledge statements generated by the understanding, Reason can no longer claim to tell us the truth about "what is." In grammatical terms, Reason does not speak to us in the indicative mood. It cannot claim that A is B, that iron is a mineral, that trees are plants, that humans are animals that think, etc. All of these statements, to be true, depend on sensuous input and our categories. Reason, however, is not mute. It speaks. If it didn't, it would be meaningless, the organ of skepticism.

When Reason speaks, however, it does not speak in the indicative, but rather in the subjunctive or the conditional mood. It does not say "what is," but rather, "what should be." What should I believe, what should I do? This is the mood of moral discourse and the discourse of belief and faith, and it is only possible beyond the limits of the scientific discourse of "what is." After Kant, the protagonists in our story of philosophy find they must espouse a different form of *logos*, a type of scientific discourse that no longer simply speaks unselfconsciously in the indicative mood of "what is." Either "what is" will have to articulate, at the same time, "what is not" (Hegel, Kierkegaard, Marx, Sartre) or it will surrender to "what must be" (Nietzsche, Kierkegaard, Marx ...).

In Kant, I cannot know whether I am free, but Reason speaks to me, in the conditional, telling me I should act as if I were free. Similarly, I cannot know whether the soul is something that transcends my earthly presence, but Reason tells me I should act "as if" it were. I cannot know whether there is an infinite, perfect being called God, but Reason tells me I should act "as if" there were. I cannot know whether there is some sense or logic to the cosmos, but Reason tells me I should believe there is. Otherwise, all knowledge becomes impossible. For how could my understanding know anything about the world if I didn't *believe* there to be a meaningful correspondence between what I experience in my mind and what actually exists in nature? So we can say that, for Kant, science is founded on Reason. That may not seem startling, until we realize that in saying this, we are also saying that science is based on freedom. This is the answer to Hume's skepticism, something that may be called rational faith. Such a faith is not relativistic or individualistic. In fact, to the extent Reason is universally shared or accessible to all human beings, we should say that rational faith is profoundly humanistic. That is its truth.

8. HEGEL

Kant's philosophy accords primacy to the moral over the theoretical domain. The limits of theoretical science lead us to discover a greater truth, that of human freedom and its faculty of pure reason. While such a solution may be elegant and satisfying on an ethical, even religious level, philosophy and indeed the human mind are unhappy with being told what can and cannot be known. There is something restless in thought itself, an inability to remain satisfied within the boundaries of its present knowledge. It is the real activity and liveliness of thought, its inability to remain still and silent and satisfied, that characterizes, more than anything else, G.W.F. Hegel's philosophy.

Beyond the imposed limits to knowledge, Kant's philosophy erects a number of other crucial barriers in the form of mutually exclusive oppositions. The theoretical domain is opposed to the moral (or practical, as it was then called) domain; understanding is opposed to Reason; belief is opposed to knowledge; science is opposed to metaphysics; and, above all, the knowing self or subject, with its empty forms and categories, seems to stand apart from the essential objects of its knowledge. This gulf is so wide and unbridgeable that all we are given to know is what we can directly glean through our senses. The thing-in-itself, as Kant calls it, i.e., the real objectivity of things, stands and will always remain beyond our knowledge. We can never know what is beyond our sensations. The reality of things-in-themselves will always remain an idea of Reason, something we should believe but can never know.

This, above all, is the barrier that rankles. The idea that there is real objectivity, real truth "out there" that can never be known, is deeply dissatisfying for the human mind and particularly, perhaps, for the German 18th-Century mind. For indeed, the philosophical period that Hegel is part of, known as German Idealism, is probably the last time in human history, and certainly the last time in this brief story, that philosophy will have the audacity, the temerity and, some might say, the folly to attempt to know the absolute truth, that which Plato sought as the Idea of the Good.

The obscene 20th-Century totalitarian regime of German National Socialism has caused some contemporary thinkers to associate the German philosophical quest for absolute truth with the expression of political absolutism. Given the recent European expressions of political totalitarianism, both Nazi and Soviet, it is understandable that much of Western postmodern thought is far more comfortable with the partial, the particular, the individual and the fragmentary than it is with anything that appears totalizing. I would add, however, that before we consider with condescension philosophy's pursuit of its greatest and oldest prize, we need to recognize that the human mind has not relinquished the quest for absolute knowledge but simply adopted a different method and language: those of mathematically driven theoretical physics. For what else is the contemporary search for the Theory of Everything (TOE), the grand unified theory that will combine knowledge of the infinitely small (quantum physics) with knowledge of the infinitely great (theory of relativity) than the search for absolute truth? Hegel represents the last moment in Western thought when this pursuit could be assigned to philosophy, not written in mathematical symbols but in the words of everyday language, regardless of how tortured this language had to become in order to approach and hold the infinite.

Earlier, I mentioned how, after Kant, philosophical language could never be the same, how *logos* could never again speak confidently in the indicative mood, simply arguing for "what is." Kant's philosophical discourse necessarily spills out of "what is," into "what should be." By doing so, it is also recognizing and alluding to "what is not." Hegel's *logos* attempts to articulate language's ultimate audacity, to express the ultimate truth of Kant's "should be," in a discourse that expresses both what is and what is not. Such a language is necessarily contradictory. However, rather than seeing contradiction as a logical dead-end, Hegel considers the opposition between what is and what is not as the very liveliness of thought itself. In the same way that Heraclitus sees the tension between life (*bios*) and death, symbolized by the drawn bow (*bios*) string, as driving forward the arrow of change, the dialectical nature of thought, in Hegel, is productive of a real process of becoming. Only that which both is and is not may become.

Just as, for Heraclitus, the flying arrow of change can be seen as the truth of the tension that drives it forward, Hegel's philosophical discourse seeks truth through the interplay of opposites. Such a truth does not eradicate the tension producing it any more than the flying arrow annuls the tension of the strung bow. Rather, the dialectical arrow, whose progression is produced by contradiction, is the on-going affirmation of the tension that produced it! This is an important point, ignored or refused by those who see Hegel's philosophy as a totalizing system that smothers all internal difference. Ultimately, Hegel's discourse seeks to reconcile essential contradictions in such a way as to conserve them within its account, to sum up the contradictory nature of life and thought in a narrative that maintains the lively tension of contradiction. This is why Hegel is so difficult to understand, and perhaps why the search for absolute truth turned to the language of mathematics.

The philosophy of a thinker who seriously intends to address absolute truth will certainly be encyclopedic. It must be a philosophy of everything, of all that humans may know as "true": of religion, art, nature, the State and of thought itself. Not since Aristotle has philosophy been so ambitious and hungry in its desire to reflect on things, and Hegel's time is perhaps the last when a well-educated, cultured individual might reasonably claim to be acquainted with the sum total of human knowledge. In this sense, Hegel's philosophy is the most daring expression of the Enlightenment's earlier *Encyclopedia* project. Indeed, his most systematic work, called the *Encyclopedia of Philosophical Sciences*, contains investigations into all the great objects of human thought.

I want to concentrate on one small corner of Hegel's encyclopedic system, a few pages from his *Phenomenology of Spirit* that pertain directly to the theme of our story: the self and its world. These few pages "have legs," as they say, significantly inspiring Marx, Sartre and others. The short passage provides a brilliant and influential solution to the problem that we saw arise, in Descartes, with the modern invention of free, self-determining subjectivity. How can something as self-contained, self-reflective, self-referencing and independent as the individual self ever know the existence of other selves? Or, in Kantian terms, how can I ever be sure those beings I sense and understand through my subjective forms and categories are themselves free subjects as I am?

Hegel was born the same year as Beethoven, 1770. After getting a virtually free education at a famous Protestant seminary in Tübingen, and doing time, as was the custom, as a children's tutor for a wealthy family in Bern, Hegel finally got a poorly paid teaching position at the University of Jena, which was, at the time, the center of German letters and science, created by the poet-philosophers Schiller and Goethe. At Jena, the pressure was on Hegel to publish something important. After a few false starts, as well as other things getting in the way, like Napoleon's military occupation of the town and Hegel's fathering of a child out of wedlock, he managed to get his *Phenomenology* published in 1807. Unfortunately, since Napoleon had closed his university, Hegel was now out of a job.

The book was intended to be an introduction or ladder up to his completely formed encyclopedic science. Never has a ladder had stranger, more challenging rungs. In fact, rather than inviting us into his system, easing us into it in a comfortable way, as introductions are usually meant to do, the *Phenomenology* is like an initiation, a trial that demands perseverance, hard work and even suffering on the part of the philosophical initiate. This is fitting because the story the book really tells is the story of the reader him or herself. It is, in Hegel's own words, the path of doubt and despair, akin to Christ's Stations of the Cross, where our illusions gradually fall away, leaving us with the highest of philosophical prizes: knowledge of ourselves, or, what is the same thing, absolute knowing. For this will be Hegel's conclusion to the *Phenomenology*, absolute knowing is nothing other than Spirit's (i.e., humanity's) knowing of itself as having passed through and experienced all previous, incomplete and unsatisfactory forms of knowledge. We may now look back on our history as the history of all the types of knowing (a.k.a. forms of consciousness) that we passed through in order to get to the point where we actually are, the point where we can now look back and grasp ourselves as what we have been.

The path we have taken no longer seems foreign to us; we, as humanity, recognize *ourselves* in our past, in the journey we have made to become who we are. The man who looks back, at the end of his life, and revisits all the trials he went through, for better and for worse, in order to become who he is (i.e., the person able to look back at his life as a whole) claims his past as his. In this way, his past experiences remain present, yet submerged, in the person he has become and in the life-story he forms. In the same way, humanity (Spirit), has now reached a point, in the *Phenomenology of Spirit*, where it can philosophically look back and recognize itself in the voyage it took getting to where it is, through all its past forms of knowing that Hegel calls forms of consciousness, and which make up what humanity has become. Hegel, whom Nietzsche saw as culminating the history of metaphysics, ultimately answers the injunction of the Oracle of Delphi, reiterated by Socrates: know thyself! In doing so, Hegel also responds to the disquieting abyss Kant postulates between subjective knowing and the thing-in-itself, the world that lies beyond our sensations. To the question, "how do I know the world exists?" Hegel answers, "because I may recognize myself in it." In this way, we can say that for Hegel, as for Socrates and Plato, recognition takes precedence over knowing.

In the *Phenomenology of Spirit*, each form of (our) consciousness that we revisit recounts a certain relationship between the knowing subject and the objectivity (or world) it knows. The book begins (we begin) with the most primitive expression of this relationship, one that is akin to how we saw it defined in Descartes: the knowing subject as the modern, isolated, independent self, the only thing certain being pure thought thinking itself. On the other hand, the object, as we saw in the chapter on Descartes, is reduced to that which the self mentally determines, an empty objectivity that I can calculate, manipulate, define or consume. Here, in this first form of knowing, called natural consciousness, the self is absolutely self-ish and the object is devoid of any substantial reality. It is only there for me. The more real I am, the less real is the world. The philosophical initiate, following the path of consciousness, begins here, and recognizes himself in this immediately natural, pre-philosophical way of looking at the world. The world is what I am not. It lies simply there before me, and ultimately, *for* me.

This form of knowing is very unsatisfying. In believing the world to be "my oyster," I have, in fact, reduced it to a kind of experiential junk food, and the same way I am not lastingly satisfied by the junk I consume, my experience of the world as simply an "other" that is there for me, leaves me feeling empty. This subjective emptiness is actually the reflection of the emptiness I projected into the world around me, and then consumed, experienced or "knew." This is the brilliant intuition of Hegel's. My sense of who I am is absolutely dependent on the world I see myself in, the world I know. A world of empty, consumable objects over which I have absolute discretion constitutes me as an endlessly empty, hungry and dissatisfied self. The Hegelian assertion that forms of knowing may be taken as societal-historical forms of consciousness is born out by the fact that we may recognize our contemporary consumer society in his portrayal of natural consciousness!

In its quest for ever more substantial knowledge and selfhood, however, the knowing subject, as philosophical novice, seeks forms of objectivity which are less empty. This philosophical dissatisfaction fuels the dialectical process that drives consciousness forward, towards more satisfying, though still contradictory, relationships between itself and the world. With each stage of the progression, the self learns from its past experience, incorporates that experience and becomes, itself, more objective or substantial. Similarly, the world that the self encounters becomes increasingly invested with the thinking activity that self has operated on it. Consequently, with each stage of consciousness or form of knowing, the subject comes to know an objectivity in which it increasingly recognizes itself. This process continues until we, as humanity, reach that ultimate form of self-recognition called absolute knowing, where the "other" is the path of our own experience, and our past experience is "us."

On this path, however, there arises a critical moment of transition, where the journey is no longer recounted as the quest of an individual consciousness but where selfhood takes on explicit social forms that move through historical moments of Western culture, like the Reformation, the Enlightenment and the French Revolution. Of course, the ultimate social form is humanity itself, recognizing itself in what it has been. The transition between the individual and the social-historical points of view occurs when the individual self comes to recognize itself in other individual selves and thus attains self-consciousness. To be aware of who I am, I must be able to recognize myself in another self, i.e., in a subject that is at the same time an object. Or, to look at this another way, according to our path, the known object has become increasingly subjective, until it reaches the point where it actually is another self. This is Hegel's famous dialectic of intersubjectivity: the original idea that I only am who I am through recognition of my selfhood in others, which is another way of saying, I am only a free self to the extent I recognize the free selfhood of others.

Hegel's theory of intersubjectivity, of self-consciousness as mutual recognition between selves, is an important response to the question that dogged both Hume and Kant, "What is the nature of self identity?" Hegel's response: I am only aware of myself as a self through recognition of the selfhood of others. My selfhood depends on other people and is therefore inherently social.

I have been looking at this point rather selfishly, from my own perspective. When I meet and know another self, however, he or she is also performing the same operation on me, namely, knowing herself in that "object" that is me. The operation we perform must be reciprocal and equal. If I simply objectify the other being, then I cannot recognize myself in that other, because that other is not then seen as a self capable of recognizing me. The result is this: to be conscious of myself, or self-conscious, I must encounter myself as another. I do this through my encounter with another self, where the other self also becomes conscious of itself as a self through its encounter with me. While this process may sound happily friendly, it is only because I am giving away its happy ending. For Hegel, the process of mutual recognition remains one of struggle, where the recognition is initially unbalanced, unequal, withheld, where one self (or group) attempts to master the other by objectifying it, enslaving it, withholding recognition of its free selfhood. Although both Marx and Sartre are inspired by this Hegelian dialectic, both are more fascinated by the struggle than by the happy outcome proposed.

In the *Phenomenology*, the struggle for recognition is first presented in abstract terms, with Hegel outlining the interplay that takes place when two selves encounter one another. To understand Hegel generally, one has to see thought or thinking as an activity that has real agency. Thinking can perhaps best be considered a type of work or activity that actually effects change on the things of the world it encounters. So, when two selves meet each other, each one takes the other, at first, as a worldly object that is there for its consideration, and sets to work on it with its thought. When I meet you for the first time, I determine you as something; I *think* you in such a way that you are something for me (e.g., a fellow professor, a student, conservative, progressive, reliable, flaky, etc.). Of course, you do the same with me, working on me with your thoughts, so as to make me what I am for you.

Thought, however, is restless; when allowed to do what it does, it constantly seeks the truth behind things and thus overcomes its own definitions. By thinking through things, I come to realize that I have not really grasped you as you are but rather that I have made you what I am. I have projected myself onto you. I have modeled you in a way that is meaningful for me. By realizing I have done this, I admit to seeing the reflection of my selfhood in you. I see that I have invested you with my selfhood. However, this position is still not very satisfying. I don't want to simply know an object that is myself. If I think things through even further, I recognize that if indeed I have recognized selfhood in you, then this selfhood must also be free, as selfhood always is. So the selfhood I recognized in you was, in truth, not really "mine," but yours. I could not have recognized my own self in you unless you were already an independent self. In the dialectic of recognition between two selves, each one performs its operation at the same time, on the other.

If this seems terribly abstract, it is because Hegel is simply setting out, in a few dense pages, an abstract outline, the "concept" as he puts it, of what has actually happened in the real world, over the last several millennia. But also, as I mentioned above, how can a language articulating a movement of becoming as the relation between what things are and are not (e.g., the selves are, for each other, both what they are and what they are not) be anything but ambiguous?

Along with Hegel's revelation that self-consciousness must involve recognition of others, we gain a powerful insight into the nature of freedom, which, since Descartes and Kant, is the very essence of modern selfhood. In recognizing the truth of your selfhood, I am also recognizing your freedom and vice versa. Real freedom cannot be purely solipsistic or individualistic. It is always tempered by mutual recognition of other people's freedom and their recognition of mine. To be free, I must be recognized as such by others, and for this to happen, I must recognize their freedom to recognize mine! Real freedom is necessarily societal.

In spite of the highly theoretical nature of this key passage from the *Phenomenology*, the struggle for mutual recognition is not meant to remain an abstract idea. It is enacted in the world, and therefore historically, in the freedom fight between an emblematic slave—who can just as easily be thought of as Greek, Roman, European, African, proletarian, woman—and his or her master. This imbalance of power is the theme of Hegel's famous master-slave dialectic, which so inspired Marx. If we are attentive to the actual path described in the *Phenomenology*, however, we see that it takes Hegel (and consciousness) another three substantial chapters of struggle to arrive at a point where humanity is historically ready for a community of free, mutually recognizing selves, in a form not actually present in any existing European State, but one to which any post-Enlightenment, democratic State may aspire in its constitution and laws. This is also the historical point where philosophical thought is ready to revisit its past and to realize that the errors it made along the way have all contributed to the truth of what it is now.

Following the unhappy ending of his stay in Jena, Hegel found employment as a newspaper editor and finally as something akin to a high school principal, a position he faithfully occupied, in Nuremberg, for nine years. It was perhaps his lifelong interest in education that allowed him to take his job very seriously, and to become involved in plans for reforms of the State education system. Perhaps getting married and raising a family (including his illegitimate son) made the socially recognized and secure position of high school principal appealing. Beyond his administrative duties, he devoted what little spare time he had to writing his second masterwork, the *Science of Logic*, whose three parts were published in 1812, 1813 and 1816. During this time, he never gave up looking for a university position, where he knew his difficult philosophy would have some chance of being understood. Finally, at the age of 48, Hegel got his first permanent, full-time university position, first in Heidelberg and then at the newly created University of Berlin; here he remained, filling lecture halls, in spite of, but also because of, the famous complexity of his thought and his renowned awkwardness of delivery, until his death from illness in 1831, the same year he published a new (and final) edition of his *Encyclopedia of Philosophical Sciences*, a study guide to absolute knowledge.

By the time of his death, Hegel had become the official philosopher of the Prussian state and one of the most renowned and influential thinkers in Europe. Although his influence waned sharply in the last half of the 19th Century, it is impossible to understand such important Continental currents as Existentialism and Marxism without knowing something about his thought. In fact, even those more contemporary philosophical tendencies that most vehemently refuse the absolute demands of Hegel's system are still reacting against him and thus proving the relevance of his demands. One of the first to reject Hegel and his all-embracing system of philosophy was the Danish philosopher, and lapsed Hegelian, Søren Kierkegaard. His efforts are truly heroic, since it is not easy to contradict a system that nourishes itself on contradiction.

9. KIERKEGAARD

n Hegel, we saw how the self, as self-consciousness, implies reciprocal recognition with others. The individual is only conscious of itself by seeing its "self" in another. This dialectical movement, the struggle for recognition, does not exist in a bubble. It is the foundation of what Hegel calls the "ethical substance" or "the State," what we might today call community or society.

The struggle for recognition can also be seen as the progression of social forms of consciousness through history. The Roman world and its social form becomes the medieval world, which is followed by the Reformation and the Enlightenment, each world representing a different form of consciousness and a different degree of social freedom or mutual recognition. Thus history is expressed in terms of the movement of consciousness or thought, to a point where humanity knows itself as free.

In Hegel, it appears that the individual only finds its meaning though its relation to otherness, through other self-consciousnesses, and ultimately through participation in social forms and their movement through world history. The individual, as such, only has significance to the extent that it participates and loses itself in this universal movement. On the other hand, the grand progression of history and thought cannot operate without the participatory activity of individuals, who fuel its movement. From the point of view of the individual, however, meaning is only achieved through sacrifice to the life of something infinitely greater, something universal, something absolute. Alone, I am nothing.

Born in 1813, Søren Kierkegaard was introduced to Hegelian thought in Copenhagen before going on, in 1841–42, to study philosophy in Berlin, under Hegel's former friend and rival, F.W.J. Schelling, who had become anti-Hegelian. Indeed, Kierkegaard begins his philosophical career struggling with the concepts and values of Hegelian thought.

Although well acquainted with Hegelianism, Kierkegaard came to react strongly against it, particularly against the idea that the existing individual only achieves meaning through participation in the generalizing category of Spirit, in humanity and its universal history. He also reacts strongly to Hegel's presupposition that the essence of humanity must be expressed as an all-embracing rational system of thought, called absolute knowledge or science. For Kierkegaard, the idea of an individual human being named Hegel constructing a system of the absolute is absurd, in the literal sense of being self-contradictory. To construct something, one must be outside the thing constructed, and so the man constructing the absolute system of science must remain outside of it. However, if the system does not include the person who constructed it, it can never be complete or absolute. You cannot have the system of absolute knowing, minus one. The system is therefore always incomplete, and the idea of an absolute system is contradictory and therefore absurd. The factitious aspect of the philosophical system is expressed in Kierkegaard's ironical pronouncements: "The Hegelian system is not yet completed and alas, now he is dead." Or, "if he were alive today, the system is so nearly complete that surely it will be ready by next Sunday."

The philosophical system is an artificial, fantastical, absurd construction. We can study the system inside and out, marvel at its wonders, but we will never find the real, living, existing individual who constructed it. In fact, it must always be incomplete because what is missing from any system of science is individual existence. Regarding the Hegelian system, it is the author himself, as an existing, living individual, who is left out of his own system of philosophy. Ultimately, this shows that individual existence is fundamentally unsystematic. Individual existence is inherently contradictory and paradoxical. The existence of the systematic philosopher is particularly paradoxical because he is attempting to lose himself in his love of the universal, in his rational system, while, at the same time, this universal system must necessarily leave him out. Hence, according to Kierkegaard, Hegel may have constructed a rational palace of crystal, but he *lives* elsewhere, impoverished, in a metaphorical thatched hut.

For Kierkegaard, the individual or subjective thinker must take the opposite path. Rather than seeking rational knowledge, he or she must seek salvation. Rather than losing himself in the system, he must leave the supposed truth of the system and seek the truth of his individual existence, which is radically unsystematic. The essence or meaning of the self's existence is not to be found through mediation and integration with otherness, through participation in the world, but rather within the self as an individual, cut off from the world. Within the existing self lies the possibility of salvation, through faith and not through reason. Despite the reassuring Christian resonance, however, Kierkegaard's ideas of faith and salvation, as we shall see, have nothing to do with the embracing succor offered by the Christian Church and its promise of an afterlife.

As well, we must take care to distinguish Kierkegaard's individual subjective thinker from the modern self as it came on the scene in Descartes. While Descartes's self is also fundamentally individual and even isolated from the opposing world of objectivity, the self is defined as a *cogito*, a thing that thinks. Reasoning is essential to the self. It *is* the self. I think therefore, I am. Thinking is the nature of the soul, and the soul is the essence and substance of the Cartesian self.

For Kierkegaard, on the other hand, the individual self exists first and thinks after. In fact, for Kierkegaard, thinking is opposed to existing. We think in order to forget we exist. We do this because existence is the experience of dread and anguish, fear and trembling. Our brief time in the world, our existence that seems so sure and necessary is, in fact, an accidental and despairingly brief break in the endless abyss of nothingness. Such a bleak view was certainly not belied by the deaths of five of his siblings and both his parents by the time Kierkegaard was 25 years of age. To forget the horror of death and the absurdity of life we may simply sink into the forgetful affairs and concerns of the everyday world, or we may preoccupy ourselves building philosophical palaces of crystal, as Hegel does. However, the terrible truth is that, first and foremost, I am. Thinking always comes later. It is this primacy of existence over thought that earns Kierkegaard his honorary status as the father of existentialism. In fact, in place of the Cartesian "I think, therefore I am," Kierkegaard insinuates, "The more I think, the *less* I am."

In spite of his promotion of individual existence over reasoning, however, Kierkegaard remains a philosopher, even a great one. There is surely something contradictory about this. Our story, up until now, has featured a series of protagonists who, in spite of all their differences, have shared one fundamental value, one premise that underlies all their work: the primacy of human reasoning. After all, reason is the very essence of *logos*, the reasonable discourse whose most excellent expression is great philosophy. Kierkegaard represents a turning point in our story, a major plot twist that will produce a type of philosophical anti-hero, philosophers who question the precept of reason while remaining philosophers, and therefore, somehow attached to the idea of reasonable discourse, of discourse that makes sense and is capable of conveying the truth about the things it refers to. How is it possible to remain attached to reasonable discourse and yet refuse reason itself?

Kierkegaard's work is the literary embodiment of this paradox. This is perfectly coherent with his philosophical vision, however. For existence is itself paradoxical, and a philosopher's writings can do nothing other than express his or her (paradoxical) existence. Even Hegel's philosophy is the expression of his (impoverished) existence. To be truthful, however, a philosophy must be as contradictory and paradoxical as the individual existence of the subjective thinker. In order to express the paradox of existence, Kierkegaard's writing employs several novel literary devices. In a way, we might say that in employing them he is responding to the same Kantian challenge that Hegel met, but in an entirely different fashion.

Faced with the impossibility of a discourse that speaks in the indicative, i.e., simply asserting or arguing the truths of metaphysical objects (God, freedom/the world, the soul), Hegel invented a form of dialectical language that constantly subverts itself to arrive at a truth that reconciles both what is and what is not. Kierkegaard's discourse does this as well. However, his dialectic is not driven by reasonable thought and arrives at no reconciliation. In fact, it is consciously ironical, both saying and not saying what is meant, in a way that is purposely unsettling for the attentive reader.

Another literary device of Kierkegaard's is his use of pseudonyms or pen names. The list of characters under whose names his writings appear includes Johannes Climacus, but also Anti-Climacus, Johannes de Silentio, Nicholas Notabene and others. Such a practice is not the same as writing anonymously, which, for political reasons, was often practiced in the 19th Century. By inventing various non-existent authors for his writings, Kierkegaard frees the writings themselves from the type of heavy correspondence to truth and demands of consistency that discourse takes on when it can be attributed to one conscious, rational self. As a good philosopher, Descartes, as Descartes, must not contradict himself. Neither should Aristotle nor Hume. Kierkegaard's pseudonymous "authors" are freed from the confining principle of identity because their own identities are many, and they don't really exist. Paradoxically, it seems the only way for writing to express the paradox of individual existence is to attribute it to a non-existent individual writer (but who really exists as Kierkegaard)!

Finally, regarding its form, Kierkegaard's discourse rarely employs argument, the fundamental expression of *logos*, of reasoning and reasoned discourse. His works tend to describe, depict, recount, state, cajole etc. but rarely do they argue from a set of established premises to a conclusion. The reader is presented with things "as they are" (by a writer who doesn't exist?) in such a way that the reader is encouraged, but not forced, to accept them, or not. Kierkegaard creates an atmosphere that invites the reader to make a choice or rather, a decision.

These literary devices certainly make Kierkegaard difficult to read. If we could make this complaint to him, he would probably say, "That's your problem. All I can do is try to set the conditions where you must choose salvation, or not." Or, he might say, "I didn't write that, Anti-Climacus did and anyway, how could anything be difficult after reading Hegel?"

The decision that Kierkegaard invites us to make is one of faith and salvation, or, as he would say, of death or life. Reasonable argument cannot lead one to make this choice. The decision, like all decisions, is ultimately un-reasonable, a leap of faith. You may stand on the rock, at the edge of the lake and run through all the arguments about why you should jump in. You are hot and the water will cool you. There are no dangers beneath the surface. The water is clean. You've done it before etc. But to leave your rock, you must finally stop reasoning and just… jump.

Appropriately enough, the contradictions of Kierkegaard's philosophy are expressed in his life. His father was an austere Lutheran minister, and young Søren rebelled against this austerity. He became a kind of dissolute dandy, an avowed pleasure-seeker, which at the time, probably didn't involve much more than staying out late, dressing well, frequenting certain cafes and flirting. He won the love of Regina Olsen, a respectable young woman, and became engaged to her. Although he claimed to be in love with her, however, he decided to break off the engagement. Instead of getting married, he went to Berlin, in 1841, to study philosophy (with Schelling) for two years.

Kierkegaard found these studies dissatisfying and returned to Copenhagen where he began his frenetic literary activity, producing 21 books in 12 years. The titles give the flavor of his work: *Fear and Trembling, The Concept of Dread, Concluding Unscientific Postscript, Sickness Unto Death*. Towards the end of his short life, he became infamous for his published attacks on organized, institutionalized religion. These aspects of Kierkegaard's life illustrate the deep contradictions that go to the core of his singular existence. While refusing the academic pursuit of philosophy, he remains profoundly philosophical. While attacking the organized practice of religion, he remains profoundly religious. The Kierkegaardian lesson is that both philosophy and religion are ultimately solitary adventures.

It is difficult to present such an anti-systematic thinker in a systematic way. One element of Kierkegaard's thought that is particularly foundational is his notion of time. By beginning with the idea of time, we can discover the important aspects of his thought, and see how they are very different from Hegel's. Also, Kierkegaard's notion of time helps us understand an important current of philosophy and literature, a current we can place him in: romanticism and the relation it implies between the individual and the world.

Kierkegaard's notion of time is very different from Hegel's. In Hegel, time can be seen as a historical progression of worldly forms of consciousness, to a point where consciousness understands itself as the summation of all that has gone before. What Hegel calls Spirit is the historical movement of human thought, in time. Humanity derives its meaning through the stages of this temporal progression. On the other hand, Kierkegaard grasps time as an unending series of instants. Each instant is the same as any other. Instants go nowhere; they are simply repeated ad infinitum, ticking by, like an old grandfather clock in an empty house.

Time, in Kierkegaard, is not a progression; it is simply an infinite series, and as such is meaningless. Ultimately, this is the time of the world. Although such worldly institutions as the State, the Church, marriage and work all promise meaningful progress (e.g., world history, personal history, professional advancement, etc.), in truth, they simply tick out a monotonous series of identical, repeating instants. This is the time the self lives in, as part of the world. Conscious of itself as living in this time, the self can feel nothing but absurdity, dread and boredom, along with the anticipation of certain death, somewhere along the inescapable series.

However, each instant also represents a possibility, the possibility of decision and choice. In each instant, the individual self has the choice of whether to remain in this unending series of futility or to decide to escape it. This is the decision Kierkegaard invites us to make. In order to make the decision pressing, he must first make us aware of the deadly futility of the time we are spending in the world.

The self that lives in worldly time and feels its boredom, often, particularly in youth, attempts to escape the monotony through pleasure. Here, each instant becomes a possibility of pleasure, of experiencing erotic, sensual ecstasy in the moment, and thereby escaping time's endless march to nowhere. Kierkegaard calls this the Esthetic stage of life. Unfortunately, sensuous pleasure is always fleeting and ultimately unsatisfying. Above all, it reveals the absurdity of time itself, because in attempting to make each instant a moment of pleasure, we are simply recreating the same monotonous, boring series we were initially trying to escape. The endless pleasures become as boring and futile and repetitive as time itself.

Fed up with the futility of pleasure-seeking, the mature individual may then choose to make sense of time by participating in something meaningful, by getting married, raising children, finding a profession, getting involved etc. One abandons the endless party of youth because one is sick of that life and feels the need for something more meaningful and lasting, something that transforms the endless series of instants into historical progressions: my marriage, children, professional life all make me feel that I am "getting somewhere" or participating in goals. This is the Ethical stage of life; it is the kind of Hegelian option that Kierkegaard had refused in eschewing marriage to Regina.

The Ethical way of living is a fiction. It is just a way of forgetting the essential meaninglessness of existence in time. It is to the ethical individual that Kierkegaard is addressing his discourse. The idea is to reveal to the cultured, mature individual, to the church-goer, the benefactor of good causes, the responsible citizen that he or she is living a lie. Time is not a meaningful historical progression. Worldly time is senseless. It is a sickness unto death.

The sole possibility of real escape is in salvation. Salvation means a leap of faith, a decision in the instant, where the mortal meets the eternal. This decision is the Religious stage of existence. In a way, it represents a return to the Esthetic stage. However, now the instantaneous ecstasy is not sensuous pleasure but rather religious, the mortal individual's possibility of encounter with the eternal in the instant. The meeting between the finite individual and the infinite is, however, a paradox. The mortal can never meet the eternal without losing itself, without being sundered to the core, which is why we must approach this leap with "fear and trembling." Kierkegaard refers ambiguously to the encounter as passion, playing off the earlier, esthetic sense of the word and the religious connotation of Christ's passion, his crucifixion and death leading to eternal life.

Similarly, the self who takes the leap of faith, loses itself. It dies to this world. It is "crucified," in order to become eternal, to save itself, although salvation is, paradoxically, a loss. We die in this life in order to live. Since this everyday life is really itself a type of waking death, dying from it opens the possibility of eternal life. Of course, again paradoxically, our eternity is only possible in the instant. It is an instant of ecstasy that is absolutely contradictory. It is, as the English Romantic poet William Blake wrote, eternity in the hour. In fact, the Religious stage of existence, as Kierkegaard ironically calls it, cannot really be a "stage" in the usual sense of something lasting in time. It is instantaneous, religious ecstasy that must necessarily leave the existing individual once again living in the world. If anything, he is now even unhappier than before. In a way, however, it no longer matters, since the individual has experienced the truth in this radically paradoxical encounter between itself and the eternal.

The Kierkegaardian encounter between the finite individual and the eternal is necessarily tragic. The individual is saved only through its loss, and its salvation takes place in a time that is neither worldly nor after-worldly. There is absolutely no promise of an after-life, which would be nothing other than the recreation of the same monotonous worldly time that was left behind in the instant. Like the hero of Greek tragedy, the religious individual remains mortal, finite, doomed. However, also like the tragic hero, in his brief time on stage, he has already lived forever.

Kierkegaard's own marginal existence wore heavily upon him. He was poor, melancholy, tortured by doubt and despair, sickly. He collapsed in the street, in 1855, and died at 42 years of age. His final words were apparently, "The bomb explodes, and the conflagration will follow."

10. MARX

ike Kierkegaard, Karl Marx's individual existence was deeply implicated in his philosophy. Both share a deep aversion for the common middle-class (bourgeois) values of their day, the solid European status quo that Hegel's participatory philosophy seems to promote. Both Kierkegaard and Marx rebelled against the generally accepted social norms, although the forms of their revolt could not have been more different. As well, both were marginal characters, living on the fringes of what was probably considered "decent society." Not coincidentally, neither was a university professor.

Karl Marx was born in the town of Trèves, in Prussia, in 1813, the same year in which Kierkegaard was born. Although born into the Jewish faith, Marx's family converted to Protestantism. He studied philosophy in Bonn, Berlin and Jena, and wrote his doctoral thesis on two ancient Greek philosophers, Democritus and Epicurus. Although Democritus was a pre-Socratic philosopher and Epicurus lived later, after Plato, they share a non-Platonic, materialist view of human nature and the cosmos. Neither of them believes in a higher metaphysical reality beyond the world, as found in Plato's otherworldly Ideas. The attraction to material reality is fundamental to Marx's later philosophy, particularly in its opposition to Hegel's idealism, which shares with Plato a fundamental belief in the primacy of thought over natural reality.

Marx edited a newspaper in Cologne, Prussia, in 1842–43, which was suppressed for its revolutionary ideas of social justice. He moved to Paris in 1843 and worked there with fellow revolutionary philosopher, Friedrich Engels, on several journals until he was again censored and asked to leave France. In Brussels, Marx and Engels worked together on another revolutionary paper and also helped form the League of the Just, a German workers' organization dedicated to communism. It was for this group that Marx and Engels wrote the *Communist Manifesto*, in which he famously invites the "workers of the world to unite," telling them they have nothing to lose but their chains.

The *Communist Manifesto* was also meant to bolster the popular uprising in France in 1848, and Marx returned there to support this short-lived revolution. Back in Cologne, Marx and Engels inaugurated yet another revolutionary paper, and this time Marx was arrested for treason. Although he was eventually acquitted, he left for London, where he wrote the first part of his famous *Das Kapital*, in the British Museum. He also continued working as a journalist, contributing to the leftist *New York Tribune*. In 1864, he formed the First International Workers' Association, an international communist organization. Marx died in 1883. The second and third volumes of *Das Kapital* were completed after his death, from his notes, by Engels.

Marx is, like Kierkegaard, an incendiary philosopher; both thinkers claim to make a bonfire or conflagration of all previous philosophy. In spite of this shared incendiary approach, Marx was also very definitely a philosopher, although he objected to being classed as such. This is because he shares with Kierkegaard, and, as we will see, with Nietzsche, a new mission for philosophy: not the quest for wisdom, but the quest for salvation. While Kierkegaard's quest for salvation is strictly personal and individual, Marx seeks to save the world. In his words: "Philosophers have up to now, only interpreted the world in different ways. Now we must change it."

Marx was well versed in Hegelian philosophy, although his reaction to Hegel is more ambiguous than Kierkegaard's. Marx refuses Hegel's rationalism, the idea that reasoning consciousness is the prime agent of historical change, and the idea that the movement of history takes place through the progress of reason, leading to an ultimate system of science. Marx also refuses the part of Hegel that seems to embed absolute knowledge in the bourgeois, Christian political State. On the other hand, Marx does adopt Hegel's notion of dialectic, the idea that contradiction and conflict produce change. The difference is that while Hegel's dialectic takes place within opposing forms of knowledge or consciousness, Marx, working with Engels, constructs a materialist dialectic.

We encountered a materialist form of thought in Thomas Hobbes, and again in a passing reference to Marx's early studies of Democritus and Epicurus. What these philosophical expressions have in common is a refusal to see the essence or meaning of the self and its world in anything transcendent or beyond the world. Such transcendence may take many forms. It may lie in Plato's other-worldly Ideas, in Descartes's idea of consciousness as a thinking substance, in Aristotle's belief in the soul as the animating form of things, or in Hegel's idea of Spirit. In all of these cases, what is transcendent can ultimately be traced back to the third player in philosophy's metaphysical drama between the self and the world: God, whether presented as such or in such forms as the Good, the Idea or the First Mover. The God question, I would argue, is ever-present in metaphysical inquiry, even when it is consciously refused and apparently absent. Such is the case with materialism. One could certainly define it as "philosophical thought that finds all meaning or essence in matter." However, the deeper character of materialism is its refusal of anything divine. Thus, there is a kind of defensive atheism in any form of materialism.

Marx's form of materialism is avowedly atheistic, although it is very different from the materialism of Hobbes (who cannot afford to do away with God entirely), Democritus or Epicurus. Whereas these materialist philosophers speak in the indicative, arguing that the truth of the human individual and the world is their thoroughly material nature, Marx sees the essence of material reality as not immediately there in nature but rather as brought about by human activity, in the form of material production or work.

Work already implies a conflictual relationship between the human agent and raw nature, which is worked upon. Hegel also subscribes to this essential conflict, at the root of his dialectic. However, whereas Hegel sees the opposition between the self and nature as productive of new forms of knowledge and consciousness, driving a historical process, Marx, true to materialist form, sees the opposition between the worker and nature as productive of ... material. He shares with Hegel the belief that the dynamics of this opposition produces a progression, and in this way, both philosophers are dialectical (in the sense of opposition producing change). Marx's philosophy, however, is one of dialectical materialism.

Marx can therefore claim, as he does, to turn Hegel on his head. With Hegel, philosophy appears to descend from the heavens onto the earth, whereas, Marx asserts, things are really the other way around. A true science of material reality has its roots in the real world. Different forms of consciousness are secondary, arising as a result of the material conditions of production. In other words, dialectical materialism is not the story of what men say or believe, but the story of what they do. What humans think, believe or say is the result of their productive or economic activity. It is not consciousness that determines human activity, but human activity that produces different forms of consciousness. This means that philosophy itself, as a specific type of consciousness, is the result of a particular form of productive, economic activity (bourgeois capitalism).

Marx's materialism refers to the economic, material production of human activity. It is dialectical in that it implies conflict, or opposition and resolution. Whereas for Hegel the dialectical opposition takes place between different forms of consciousness, for Marx the opposition is between types of economic productivity. Since different types of economic activity produce different social classes, the dialectical conflict actually takes place between different classes: slaves versus free citizens; serfs versus barons; indentured workers versus the guilds; the factory workers versus the bourgeois capitalists. The historical movement produced by the dialectic of materialism is the story of class struggle, the story of oppressed workers in the struggle against their oppressors.

Historically, the struggle begins with the master-slave relationship of ancient Greece and Rome, moves through the feudal period of serfdom, and through the period of tradesmen and guilds, to modern bourgeois capitalist society. Modern, industrial, capitalist society is the outcome of a long history of conflict between opposed economic classes. This is not a conflict inherent in human nature, as we saw in Hobbes, where man is naturally nasty and selfish. In Marx, the struggle is dialectical in that it follows a kind of material logic, the logic of capital, of profit-seeking economics. In other words, profit or capital follows its own economic law which has determined all aspects of human history, understood as the history of class struggle. The material logic of history is the ever-increasing concentration of capital in the hands of ever-fewer people.

In modern capitalism, the process has accelerated. Competition for profit causes bigger producers to absorb smaller ones, a process that moves inexorably towards a position where capital is concentrated in the hands of very few, the bourgeois capitalists, while all others are reduced to the class of the proletariat. Proletarians are workers whose labor has become a simple commodity, a cost of production. They no longer work for their own benefit. Rather, their work is simply a factor in the accumulation of profit in the hands of the ever-richer and fewer capitalists. In Marxist terms, proletarians are workers who have become alienated from the products of their labor.

Work is inherently, for Marx as for Hegel, a significant endeavor through which the worker derives meaning. For both Hegel and Marx, the individual worker is meant to recognize him or herself in the fruits of the labor. The ideal model, for both philosophers, is the artisan or the artist. I invest myself (i.e., my knowledge, training, personality) into the thing I work, which is recognized by me and others as the real result of *my* work. In capitalist society, Marx claims, the proletariat has become separated from his labor. His labor is simply a commodity. Working within the industrial chain of production, the worker can no longer recognize himself in the work he has invested in the product. The worker is simply a commodity in modern production. As a commodity, he is prized entirely for his cheapness. The more he produces, the cheaper his labor is, and hence the less actual value he has. However, at the same time, his cheap labor adds to the market value of what he produces. This added value becomes the profit, or capital, taken by the factory owner, the capitalist. The idea of cheap labor as producing "surplus value" is revolutionary. It means the worker's labor becomes the capitalist's profit. As a fundamental human activity, work has lost its meaning. The more it is financially devalued, the more profit is created, but not for the worker.

A compelling image of surplus value and worker alienation is presented in Charlie Chaplin's early industrial depiction of the hapless worker on the assembly line, in his film *Modern Times*. Here, work has been reduced to a repetitive, absurd pantomime, devoid of all meaning and de-humanizing to the extent the worker literally is in danger of being absorbed into the machine. On Marx's reading, every repetitive gesture the worker accomplishes on the product as it moves by him or her on the assembly line adds to the profit the factory owner derives from the finished product, to the extent the worker in-put is always undervalued. If such early industrial images seem dated and no longer pertinent, one merely has to look further off-shore to discover more contemporary and exotic enactments of Chaplin's portrayal of worker alienation.

According to Marx, the only satisfaction and freedom the proletariat can achieve is in eating, drinking and procreating, i.e., in animal satisfactions, and this fact has its own economic logic. Familiar with the industrial age mores of the British worker, Marx saw how the laborer is induced to spend a significant amount of his (always minimal) salary in the pub, how the pub closes early enough to get him home, where the only satisfaction available is likely sexual intercourse and just enough sleep before delivering himself onto the factory steps before the morning whistle. Capitalist logic means the worker must procreate, must produce enough children to keep him living precariously on the edge of poverty, while at the same time supplying the system with more proletarians (i.e., cheap, child) labor. Capitalist logic also demands worker insecurity, instability, precariousness, constant fear of unemployment, where the only thing plentiful is the number of surplus, unemployed workers willing and able to take your job or to do it more cheaply.

The logic of capitalism, amassing ever-greater profits in fewer and fewer hands, means that new markets must be created for the ever-increasing (and ever-cheaper) production of goods. Capitalism must convert other lands and cultures, not only to make them desire to consume products that traditionally they had no need or desire for, but also to supply the system with more cheap, off-shore labor.

We can certainly recognize elements of our own economic reality in Marx's description of capitalism, even though we generally refuse such terms as "proletariat," "bourgeois" or "capitalist." Even the term "worker" is generally substituted for such edifying denominations as "coordinator," "associate," "technician," "barista" etc. Of course, Marx did not see his dialectic ending in the triumph of capitalism as we might witness it today. Rather, capitalist society eventually contradicts itself and brings about its own demise. This happens in several ways.

First, the logic of capital, where profit accumulates in fewer and fewer hands, means that eventually virtually all capital will be held by one capitalist or by a very small group. When this happens, no one else will be able to consume the ever-increasing amount of products produced by the system. Over-production will come to smother consumption and the system will begin to fail. At the same time, the means of transportation and communication that capitalism must develop, in order for it to move goods, capital and labor, brings about over-arching centralization that also facilitates communication among the world proletariat, allowing it to form a vast revolutionary network. Today, the Internet appears as both a business-enhancing instrument, promoting the exchange of goods and capital, creating new possibilities of consumption, but also as a network facilitating communication for various counter-cultural, revolutionary, even terrorist groups. Similarly, Marx saw rail lines and the telegraph as inherently ambiguous. The collapse of bourgeois capitalism and the triumph of the proletariat are therefore dialectically (materially) inevitable, in the same way Hegel's logic predicts the eventual overturning of the master by the slave.

The end of class struggle, for Marx, does not take place in the triumph of the proletariat, however, but in the birth of a classless "communist" society where the economic definitions of proletariat and capitalist disappear. Here, labor will be carried out on a voluntary basis, in the way we tend to associate with craftsmanship or artistic endeavor, where the worker/artist once again recognizes him or herself in the thing produced. One may decide to go hunting or fishing in the morning, and then be free to do some other work in the afternoon or to leisurely spend time in discussion with one's friends or family. Such leisure is possible because there is no need to produce ever-greater profits for ever-richer capitalists, and modern machine technology can do much of the boring drudgery work that capitalism assigned to the under-valued, alienated worker. Machines were meant to liberate humanity, not to enslave it.

Such a utopian vision may strike us as naïve, unrealistic or passé. We may be tempted to associate the communist ideal with life in the former Soviet Union and the collectivist nightmare of Stalinist totalitarianism. It is important not to forget, however, that Marx's ideal is, above all, one of social justice and social freedom, where we also find a genuine quest for individual happiness. Seeing such human possibilities as antithetical to the frenetic compulsion for profit, consumption and cheap labor is surely something we can relate to.

The logic of dialectical materialism does not mean, for Marx, that the philosopher should simply sit back and wait for the end of class struggle. By replacing the traditional goal of philosophical wisdom with that of salvation, Marx engenders a new role: the thinker as militant, as activist. In concrete terms, this means making the proletariat conscious of his or her condition or class. Once again, it is not enough to interpret, we must transform. Thus, Marx's philosophy should not only be seen in his writings, but in his personal involvement in such movements as the First International Workers' Association, in 1864, or in his journalistic activity. In fact, Marx provides a model for the 20th-Century figure of the militant intellectual, above all in France, where the activities and writings of philosophers such as Jean-Paul Sartre or Michel Foucault may be considered socially and politically relevant.

Although this model of philosophical involvement is, with a few notable exceptions, foreign to the English-speaking world, where thinkers are often viewed as idealistic bumblers with no sense of the real world and who are best left in their academic ivory towers, the philosopher who has reflected on justice and the good often feels the vocation to social involvement. In the same way, the liberated prisoner from the depths of Plato's cave, having experienced the ideal light, feels called upon to return to the land of shadows, even though his enlightenment is viewed by his former captives as ridiculous and perhaps dangerous.

In a story about the self and its world, Marx opens up a new plotline: the possibility of an active, integrated relation, where we may actually transform the world we live in through real political involvement. Indeed, on Marx's reading, all involvement (or non-involvement) is political, whether we are conscious of the fact or not. Finally, it is because all Marx's philosophical activity is aimed at making us conscious of the truth of our actual condition in the world, that he remains, in spite of his own protestations, a true philosopher.

11. NIETZSCHE

Friedrich Nietzsche is our third incendiary philosopher. Like Kierkegaard and Marx, Nietzsche claims to make a bonfire of the philosophical tradition, and to transform humanity in the future. We may easily put Kierkegaard's reported last words in Nietzsche's mouth: "A bomb explodes. The conflagration will follow." In a similar vein, although he died in 1900, Nietzsche claimed that he would be the philosopher of the following century, of the 20th Century. In many ways, like Kierkegaard, he remains our contemporary.

As was the case with Kierkegaard and Marx, Nietzsche abandons philosophy's traditional search for wisdom, seeking instead the salvation of humanity through its transformation. This, of course, implies that humanity is in peril or sick. In Kierkegaard, this sickness is a fundamental condition of being human, of existing as a human being in time. In Marx, the sickness is the inequality and injustice of modern industrial society. For Nietzsche, the sickness is the result of 2,000 years of Judeo-Christian religion and Western philosophy. In fact, it is the very story we have been following, from Socrates to Hegel that has made humanity mortally ill.

Friedrich Nietzsche was born in Saxony, Germany, in 1844, and, like Kierkegaard, was the son of a Lutheran minister. His father died when Nietzsche was five years old, and he was brought up by his mother. At the Gymnasium (a high school emphasizing classical studies) he studied Greek and Roman philology (the study of language and literature) and Christian theology. He continued his studies at Bonn and Leipzig, where he read, and was greatly impressed by, Schopenhauer's *The World as Will and Representation*. Nietzsche was a brilliant, promising scholar and became a professor at the University of Basel in 1869, without having done a doctorate.

After the Franco-Prussian war of 1870, where he volunteered as a nurse, he returned to his teaching, in Switzerland. Here, he met and became friends with the opera composer Richard Wagner. He and Wagner initially shared an enthusiasm for Schopenhauer's pessimistic philosophy, the idea that the world is pure illusion (representation), and that human will is blind and the source of suffering; consequently, only by extinguishing our will through a kind of Buddhist self-abnegation, can we contemplate the truth in the form of Ideas, understood in a quasi-Platonic sense. Although Nietzsche shared with Schopenhauer and Wagner a strong feeling for the sickness and futility of his epoch, and of his world, he later came to react strongly against what he saw as his fellow intellectuals' morbid nihilism.

Nietzsche continued teaching at Basel until 1879, becoming increasingly disenchanted with the world of academe and its denizens. During this time, however, he wrote his ground-breaking *The Birth of Tragedy*, originally dedicated to Wagner. This work renewed the way classical philology was practiced and the way the Ancient Greeks were considered. This reinterpretation of the Ancients is important because Western civilization has always defined itself with reference to the Greeks. They have always been part of our identity, of our understanding of who we are (e.g., the story you are reading begins with them). Although it may be less true today, in the 19th Century, a cultured individual understood that he or she was very much the result of two major traditions: the Greco-Roman and the Judeo-Christian. Nietzsche saw that our modern identity is a result of how we relate ourselves to these traditions, although his appraisal of these cultural influences and our contemporary identity was highly original.

In *The Birth of Tragedy*, Nietzsche contrasts two opposed Greek tendencies, which he attaches to two different gods: Dionysus and Apollo. Traditionally, in Greek philology, Dionysus is the god of wine, revelry, chaos and death whereas Apollo is the god of order, art, reason, light and life. Greek tragedy was, above all, defined as Apollonian, an art where, following Aristotle's predominant interpretation, salutary catharsis leads to the restoration of order and balance. Nietzsche reverses these accepted connotations, drawing upon the mythological tradition according to which Dionysus is the god who is twice born of Zeus. According to this tradition, Dionysus, upon his death, is cut into pieces and consumed in order to be reborn as a chaotic life force, unbridled, dangerous and destructive in its power. On this reading, Apollo, the sun-god of order, stands *opposed* to life. Thus, whereas traditionally Apollo represented life and Dionysus death, now the roles are reversed.

Greek tragedy, the highest form of Greek culture, had hitherto been understood as an essentially Apollonian expression, where the death of the hero represents a return to order. Now, however, the Apollonian element represents a deadly, repressive influence on Dionysian life as a chaotic revel. On Nietzsche's appraisal, the historical progression of Greek tragedy, from the early works of Aeschylus, through Euripides, to Sophocles is one of decadence, exemplified in the decline of the life-affirming, Dionysian role of the chorus, in the early tragedies, to its more orderly, moral character in later works. Later tragedy has become an Apollonian expression that is anti-life, against the Dionysian affirmation of life. The dynamic, contradictory, indeed "dialectical" relationship between order, art, death and life, which first surfaces in the brilliant *Birth of Tragedy*, remains the theme of Nietzsche's body of work.

In 1879, Nietzsche leaves his teaching post because of "illness." He suffered from migraines, rheumatism and perhaps syphilis, which he had been treated for in Leipzig. Interpreted philosophically, sickness and health display a dialectical complicity; as with life and death, they are not to be held separate. Indeed, Nietzsche revels in his bouts of sickness because they are followed by periods of good health where he feels the intoxicating return of raw, invigorating life. Similarly, just as art may be evaluated according to whether it represents a Dionysian affirmation of life or the opposite, so may art represent either an expression of sickness or of health.

Having left academe, he became a wanderer and a writer, living for periods in Italy, Switzerland and southern France. During his wanderings, he wrote such works as *Beyond Good and Evil*, *The Genealogy of Morals*, the *Twilight of the Gods* and *The Antichrist*. He also planned to marry the fascinating and philosophical Lou Andreas Salome, who eventually, and wisely, refused him. Spending the summer in the Alps, in 1881, he had a kind of illumination: the intuition of "the eternal return of the same." This experience inspired his later book, *Thus Spake Zarathustra*. In 1889, he suddenly went mad. After being found talking to a horse in the street, he was locked up, and then brought home, where he was looked after by his mother and sister for ten years until he died, in 1900. By then, his writings had made him famous.

Unfortunately, his sister, who was married to an anti-Semite whom Nietzsche despised, edited his unfinished manuscripts to produce a book called *The Will to Power*, in such a way as to make Nietzsche look like an inspiration for the German Third Reich, a debt that Hitler later commemorated, laying a wreath on the sister's tomb and pronouncing her the Grandmother of Nazism. How was she able to edit her brother's work in this way? Part of the answer is in the form of Nietzsche's writing. Like Kierkegaard, Nietzsche could not adopt the form of *logos* employed by the philosophical tradition he rejects, including the systematic dialectical discourses of Hegel and Marx.

Instead, Nietzsche adopts the aphorism, the relatively short and pithy literary fragment, as the preferred form of discourse. This language trope allows him to appear, again like Kierkegaard, thoroughly unsystematic, while maintaining an underlying, although ironical, coherence. What I mean by this is that the contradictions that Nietzsche revels in are in fact dialectical, in the Kierkegaardian sense: they are meant to express the contradictory nature of both existence and thought, and to create an environment that puts the reader to the test. Again, what is at stake is a type of salvation for the reader, through an event of self-loss, although in Nietzsche we are definitely not dealing with a Christian salvation!

In any case, the fragmentary, contradictory nature of the aphorisms makes them easy to interpret in ambiguous ways. For example, Nietzsche's statements about Jews or about women can be selected or read in such a way as to make him appear crudely anti-Semitic or sexist, if one edits out his blistering condemnations of both anti-Semites and modern, European males! However, perhaps some of the responsibility for its misuse lies in Nietzsche's philosophy itself, the same way part of the responsibility for the Stalinist Soviet Union may lie with Marx. In fact, the problem might arise from a fundamental contradiction in the project common to both, the project of saving humanity while at the same time undermining the foundation on which their concept of humanity rested: the Western philosophical tradition.

For Nietzsche, the entire history of philosophy, particularly from Socrates and Plato, is a gigantic lie. Why? Because it invents something called the Truth. The concept of Truth is a man-made invention, meant to mask or escape from the essential untruth of life. If Truth is that which is eternal, unchanging, non-self-contradictory, then it is the opposite of what life actually is: a Dionysian revel of contradiction and change. As Nietzsche's favorite pre-Socratic philosopher, Heraclitus, put it, in life we are parcels of death and death is the principal outcome of life. The idea of an eternal, unchanging Truth allows us to forget this terrifying contradiction.

Although Nietzsche does enquire into truth, his interest is not immediately epistemological. The question about how science can know the truth, the question that motivated Descartes and Hume, does not, in itself, interest Nietzsche. His question is rather, "why did we invent this concept of truth?" To put it another way, "What is this Will to truth in us?" How did it get there? And most important, "What is the value of this Will to truth?" Why not rather untruth? Perhaps untruth is of greater value to life.

The idea of life is the most fundamental element in Nietzsche's philosophy, against which all else is measured or evaluated. It has been said that each great philosopher has one big idea, which he or she articulates in interesting, original and coherent ways. Such big ideas are often fundamental intuitions, appearing to our philosophers as immediately true and to us as the presuppositions or premises of their main arguments. Plato's intuition might be the reality of Ideas; Descartes's might be consciousness as reflection; Kant's might be the universality of Reason; Hegel's might be the agency of thinking. Nietzsche shares with his two fellow incendiary philosophers deep intuitions that reject metaphysical abstraction (i.e., Hegelian idealism) in search of the reassuringly real. Thus, Kierkegaard's fundamental intuition is real individual existence; Marx's is real material production and Nietzsche's is life. Of course, since there is nothing more real in the *concepts* of existence or production or life than there is in the concepts of reflection, reason and thought, our three reality-seekers cannot help but fall back into the history of concept-production they seek to escape, and which we know as philosophy! Perhaps Marx's personal, political involvement represents the best possibility for a non-conceptual philosophical activity.

For Nietzsche, the question of truth and untruth is finally: "Which is of greater value to Life?" Philosophers have usually claimed that everything has its opposite, and so the same must be true with values. Philosophers have always made the claim that if good is a value, then what is bad is not. Similarly, since truth appears to be undeniably a value, then deception is not. However, what if the will to delusion, to selfishness and cupidity should be of a higher and more fundamental value for life? As Nietzsche writes in *Beyond Good and Evil*, "The falseness of an opinion is not for us any objection to it ... The question is, how far an opinion is life-furthering, life-preserving, species-preserving, perhaps species-rearing ... and we are fundamentally inclined to maintain that the falsest opinions are the most indispensable to us."

We illustrate Nietzsche's point every day, in our lives. We forget the fact we are going to die. We lie to ourselves that we are not essentially animals destined to disappear either suddenly and unexpectedly or through long and painful illness. Nonetheless, while we may be living a giant lie, our self-deception is actually rather creative and is certainly life-enhancing. To be constantly, painfully aware of our mortality would probably bring about a morbid state of depression and sickness.

The true philosophical question is one of value, not truth. Opinions or ideas should be evaluated, and the criterion for that evaluation is not their truth but their ability to enhance or depress life. In fact, the will to truth may actually be life-sapping, morbid. The ability to deceive oneself and others is perhaps what is best for life. In this light, the whole history of philosophy, of the desire for wisdom and truth, may be life-threatening. If that is the case, why did we invent this "will to truth?" Why did we invent something that is anti-life?

The question, for Nietzsche, is ultimately a moral one, because the question of value is a moral question (not a moralistic one). The will to truth rests upon the question of good and evil, and the belief, stretching back to Socrates and Plato, that the Truth is good and the Good is the Truth. Consequently, the question about where "the will to truth" comes from can only be answered by examining its roots in "the will to good." Nietzsche therefore asks the question, "What intrinsic value do the concepts of good and evil have in themselves?" Where did they come from? And since value always must be measured in relation to life, this is how good and evil must be evaluated. "Are good and evil a symptom of the ... degeneration of Human Life? Or, in them, do we find the will of Life, its courage, its self-confidence, its future?" In *Beyond Good and Evil*, Nietzsche traces the secret history or "genealogy" of the inventions or lies known as good and evil.

According to Nietzsche, in humanity, there is a master morality and a slave morality. Initially, in an undefined historical period, probably inspired by the Homeric myths, the master morality is dominant. This is an aristocratic morality, which literally means "government by the best." Here, such qualities as physical strength, loyalty, courage and pride are celebrated. The aristocratic masters are like Homeric warrior heroes, particularly, perhaps, in the mold of Achilles and Ajax. They are strong and life-affirming, arrogant and instinctive. They are not afraid of death because it will probably come in combat and will thus reaffirm their qualities of bravery and strength.

For this type of warrior morality, "good" refers to the aristocratic values of strength, loyalty, courage etc. "Bad" simply refers to "all those who are not us," to all those who are not aristocratic. These bad others are defined negatively. They are not noble because they are weak, tired, stunted, hesitant and dependent. Above all, remarks Nietzsche, they are

possessed and driven by resentment. They are deeply envious and resentful of their aristocratic masters, and are obsessed by their jealousy. Why them and not me? Nietzsche asks
us to suppose that such beings invented a morality. What would it look like?

The weak slaves would invent a morality that would curtail the power of their masters, whom they fear. They would invent a morality that would emasculate their masters, so the slaves would no longer have to fear them, a morality that saps the aristocrats
of their best-loved qualities, to make them doubt themselves, to turn their cruelty onto
themselves, to live in fear and servitude. The slaves therefore invent Christian morality and values. These are the exact reverse of the warrior values. Humility replaces pride;
penitence replaces cruelty; patience replaces action; meekness replaces valor; death (and
the after-life) replaces life. Virtue, which had been originally identified as a masculine
strength, has been replaced by what was now considered the feminine virtue of chastity,
and its essential sterility.

The masters are forced to adopt these new values, and become part of the herd they
formerly dominated. The slave morality, with its values born of resentment, are the values
of Christian morality; they are fundamentally designed to protect the weak, tired, fearful
and sick from the strong, natural masters. As one of its values, Christianity adopted the
Platonic ideal of Truth. Whereas the aristocrat, the blond brute, as Nietzsche unfortunately calls him, saw truth in terms of loyalty and strength of purpose ("true," in the sense
of straight), the slave morality promotes the idea of truth as otherworldly and ideal. Like
Plato's Ideas or the Christian God, Truth is "out there," beyond; as such, it is the object
of contemplation, study and prayer rather than of action.

The goal of genealogy is to show historically how we became who we are today, to
diagnose our sickness and perhaps to indicate a possible cure. While Nietzsche says that
"today" the two moralities are mixed, even in particular individuals, Western civilization
is essentially symptomatic of slave morality, of the morality of the herd. Modern man,
for Nietzsche, is "the last man," a decadent endpoint. Modern democracy is a symptom
of a generalized sickness and we are sick because we are the result of 2,000 years of slave
morality that was itself invented by the "unhealthy." The philosophical search for truth
is another symptom, part of a great lie invented by the weak.

If we stop here, we are left with a one-dimensional and potentially dangerous presen-
tation of Nietzsche's thought, one that might fuel dark, puerile fantasies of heroic supe-
riority, to be played out in teenage bedrooms, on the Internet or, in the most tragically
stupid cases, in the real world, with guns. We have witnessed a lunatic named Hitler mold
his fringe political party to such a Nietzschean caricature in order to convince a humili-
ated nation that its destiny depended on rediscovering its past martial strength and mas-
tery, by purifying itself of all elements of weakness and disease.

Such a shallow view is not, however, a faithful one. Nietzsche's thought is much
more nuanced, and even contradictory. He certainly does not promote a return to aristocratic, warrior values, nor to a world dominated by brutes. In fact, the lies invented by
the slave morality can be seen as representing the greatest artistic achievement of human-

ity. Judeo-Christian morality and Western post-Platonic philosophy and their lies of the Good and the True are the most spiritual artistic creations of mankind. Significantly, these are the creations of the downtrodden, the "weak"; brutes create nothing. Further, one could say that in artfully triumphing over their masters, the weak have proven themselves, ultimately, to be more powerful, to have a greater will to power than those they have tamed. Further still, the artistic productions of the weak (religion, philosophy, culture) are infinitely more interesting for the Nietzschean thinker than is the bloody, stupid world of the "blond brutes."

The genealogy does not, however, leave us feeling comfortable and secure about ourselves and our moral world. We realize that this world and its values have been created and, to the extent we subscribe to them, created by us. Therefore, if we are not happy with our world, if we feel that it is somehow decadent, false or empty, it is we who have made it that way and only we who might change it.

If there is salvation in Nietzsche's philosophy, it begins with the shocking acceptance that "God is dead." This famous pronouncement means that Christianity as a real, living values-producing religion is defunct. The problem is that few people realize it. They continue to stumble on, constantly repeating, reworking, re-juggling the same slave morality, oblivious of the fact that it has run its course, that it is no longer of value and that it is sapping us of any possibility of inventing something new. For this is the greatest legacy of Nietzsche: if humanity were artistic enough to produce such great creations as Goodness and Truth, it would be capable of creating a new morality, one that is life-enhancing. In other words, not only must we realize that "God is dead," we must also recognize our responsibility in His demise. Only thus can we recognize our ability to create new gods.

Such a demand takes the form of that ambiguous Nietzschean figure, the *Übermensche* (translated as superman, on condition that "man" is taken in the generic sense of human and thus includes woman) and is related to his key idea of the eternal recurrence. The superman embodies the possibility of a new morality. It is the fusion of Dionysus and Apollo. The superman is both life-affirming and creative, but is also both man and woman, father and mother, slave and master, truth and lie. The eternal recurrence provides a clue to deciphering this hypothetical creature.

The superman lives in time, while living fully in the "now." He or she does this by being conscious of eternity. For Nietzsche, and this was perhaps his illumination in the Alps, the finite world and its time are limited in their possible configurations, while eternity is infinite. Since there is only so much matter and a finite range of possibility for its interaction or occurrence in the universe, and the universe stretches out over eternity, worldly occurrences must recur, not just once, but ... eternally. This is what the Demon whispers in *Zarathustra*, "This life that you now live and have lived, you will have to live it again and countless times again .... " Such is the test of the superman: to be able to answer the affirmative "yes!" to each "now" in one's life, knowing that each moment will come again and again and again.

The superman implies the possibility of a totally life-affirming life. The Western "last man" necessarily fails this test. The superman must "come along"; he or she is not yet here, must yet be born. Rather than conjuring nightmarish visions of a coming master race, a more reasonable and deflationary account of the superman's genesis can be found in Nietzsche's belief in youth's Dionysian renewal of possibilities and his passionate interest in a system of education that is invigorating rather than stultifying. Finally, we may see Nietzsche's superman as the embodiment of pure, unfettered possibility.

Nonetheless, we can't help feeling that Nietzsche also poses the idea of the eternal return as a hypothesis that even we, decadent "last men," might use, a challenge to see our lives as our own creations, to ask ourselves if indeed we can affirm our lives to the point where we would live every instant over again eternally. While such a challenge forces us to recognize that our lives are our responsibilities, there is also something liberating about Nietzsche's "philosophy of the hammer," as he calls it. Such a philosophy enjoins us to evaluate our inherited values, not as foreign to us but rather as our own creations. For only then may we participate in the creation of new values.

To the objection that such questioning and creation are dangerously relativistic or destabilizing, Nietzsche would probably answer that philosophy is meant to be danger-ous. Unfortunately, there is no better illustration of the reality of these dangers than those engendered by Nietzsche's philosophy itself.

12. SARTRE

Kierkegaard, Marx and Nietzsche have at least one thing in common, besides refusing the philosophical tradition: a visceral disdain for bourgeois (i.e., middle-class) existence. Everyday life of the status quo is either meaningless, unjust or a symptom of decadence. Such a state of affairs obviously has repercussions for the individual. He or she can no longer find meaning by simply acting in the world, by participating in the affairs of the world, as was the case for Hegel. Common activities like finding a career, getting married, raising a family, getting involved in the community appear empty and artificial. For our three incendiary philosophers, if the individual is to find meaning, he or she must stand against the reigning, bourgeois way of the world. In doing so, however, the self is in danger of alienation and isolation.

If there is no meaning (essence) to be found in the world, the solitary individual must find it in himself. For Descartes, this is not a problem because the self is always already isolated and has to look no further for essence than within his own rational soul. The thinking soul of the individual *is* its essence. When I think myself, I discover my meaning: to be a thing that thinks. A reflexive return into the self is a discovery of meaning.

However, the soul as an essential, foundational substance implies the existence of God, the creator of the soul and guarantor of truth in my reasoning. Now that God is dead, for both Marx and Nietzsche, the rational soul becomes meaningless. Even in Kierkegaard, who certainly believes in God, the inner, individual soul is no longer essential or meaningful. In my instantaneous and tragic encounter with God, my individual self is sundered to the core and annihilated. In this context, the idea of an eternal, substantial soul within me is discarded. Starkly put, this is the modern situation. God is dead. The everyday world is a lie. The self is meaningless. Reason is no longer the path to salvation.

At the same time, however, the legacy of these philosophers is their quest for sal-vation, the belief that philosophy should change things or hasten changes, either in the individual or in the world. The quest for salvation is also part of our contemporary situ-ation, which can perhaps now be understood as a search for lost essence or meaning. It is into this context that Jean-Paul Sartre and modern existentialism arise.

Sartre's most important philosophical work, *Being and Time*, was published with the senseless butchery of World War II as its backdrop, during the Nazi occupation of France, and only 25 years after the end of the other "war to end all wars," in which Europe had lost millions of "souls." In such a historical context of deadly absurdity, it is easy to under-stand how the modern situation could become very real: God is dead (how could He per-mit such butchery?), the world is a lie (governments are bent on murdering their citizens), the self is insignificant (death is mass-produced), and reason does not lead to salvation (it produces technologies of mass destruction). Sartre's existentialism can be defined as the quest for individual meaning in a world that has become thoroughly senseless.

Sartre was the consummate Parisian intellectual. He was born in Paris in 1905 and, after a full and turbulent life, he died there in 1980. He was educated at the famous *grande école* for literature and philosophy, *L'école normale supérieure*, then at the University of Fribourg (Switzerland) and the French institute in Berlin. In 1929, he met the philoso-pher Simone de Beauvoir who became his life-long companion and associate.

He passed the highly competitive *Agrégation* exam, which allowed him to teach philosophy in high schools while writing a thesis and preparing for a career as a univer-sity professor. Historical events conspired to ensure this would never happen. Instead, the World War II broke out and Sartre was captured and imprisoned by the Germans, as were many French soldiers. Released under the German Occupation, he taught high school and wrote his defining philosophical work, *Being and Nothingness*, which was pub-lished in 1943.

Following the war, he gave up teaching and founded a political, literary magazine, *Les temps modernes*. He also turned to writing novels (*Nausea*, the trilogy *Paths of Freedom*) and plays (*The Flies, No Exit*). Like most post-war European intellectuals, he was a com-munist, although following a visit to the Soviet Union in 1954, he became as critical of Soviet communism as he was of U.S.-style capitalism. In 1960, he published his other monumental, though less remarkable, philosophical treatise, *The Critique of Dialectical Reason*, a work that attempts to reconcile individual freedom with the political realm through group revolutionary activity. His later writings are in literary and political criti-cism, such as his biography of the 19th-Century writer, Gustave Flaubert. In 1964, Sartre refused the Nobel Prize for literature, saying it would compromise his independence.

Sartre's life is one that expresses freedom and political activism, in the tradition of the intellectual that I described in the chapter on Marx. Fittingly, these are the themes of Sartre's philosophical existentialism, where, through free action, one gives meaning to one's life. How does this work?

To sum up existentialism, it may be best to begin with Sartre's own description of the philosophy as one where existence precedes essence. This is the opposite of what we find in the philosophical tradition, where the inner essence of a thing (that which makes a thing what it is) determines the existence of a thing (the way it actually is). The essential "horseness" of the horse determines that it *be* one. The essence of an evergreen tree determines that it will *be* an evergreen by not losing its foliage in the winter. If I am essentially a good person, I will do the right thing. If you are essentially brave, you will behave bravely. Even in Descartes, the first modern philosopher, we find this order. My essence is thinking, therefore I must exist as a thing that thinks.

As we have seen, essence is also related to meaning. The inherent essence of something gives it its meaning. Discovering the truth about something involves discovering its inner essence. If we discover that, then we know it, although we may use other terms than essence. We may refer to finding out "what makes something/someone tick," or, we may think of essence in terms of an inner nature. Things are what they are because their nature makes them that way. In their nature, we know them. Thus, investigation into the human genome is seen as a way to discover our inner nature in order to know who we really are, to discover our truth, our meaning, our soul.

The reference to soul is significant; it allows us to see how we tend to see essence as something unique and lasting, even eternal, even though the accompanying existence may change. A person is said to go through many changes in a lifetime, from child, to idealistic adolescent, to optimistic entrepreneur, to disillusioned middle manager, to becalmed retiree ... Yet we assume an underlying permanent nature/essence/soul ensures identity through the changes. However, if God is dead and the world is meaningless, how can we have an inner soul or meaning?

In reversing the relationship between essence and existence, Sartre supplies an answer to the problem of missing essence, of missing meaning. I create my essence through the way I exist. However, this applies exclusively to human beings. Whereas an object is always immediately caught up in its own nature or essence, the human individual (as self-conscious) is alone capable of real *existence*. This is because human beings are free *to be*. Other beings simply *are*. We might say that they subsist without truly existing. In Sartre's adopted Hegelian terms, human consciousness is "for-itself," whereas other beings/things are "in-itself." For example, a chair is a chair because it is "in-itself" a chair. Its essence is to be a chair and that is all it can be. It subsists as a chair. It does not *exist*, as a free human being does.

Human existence, unlike the subsisting object, has the possibility to determine itself. It can be "for-itself" and not just "in-itself." This is because human consciousness is *essentially* nothing. There is no essential human soul predetermining what I am. I have no pre-existing essence other than my not having an essence, and this nothingness is my freedom. I am not predetermined by an inner soul/nature/essence and so I am free. Because it is essentially nothing, human consciousness is essentially free to determine itself through its actions.

Part of the pleasure of reading Sartre derives from his enormous literary skill at animating the type of conceptual abstraction found in the paragraph above with convincing depictions of imaginary scenarios. He illustrates his idea of freedom as essential nothingness by asking us to imagine ourselves walking on the edge of a cliff, experiencing the familiar feeling of anxiety, that we will somehow be drawn over the brink, in spite of the fact that our footing is secure, there is no wind etc., and we are objectively in no danger. The anxiety we feel is that of our pure nothingness, of our pure freedom, a truth we bring to light by simply answering the question, "What is stopping me from throwing myself over the cliff?" Nothing. This nothingness is the anxious experience of my pure freedom.

Essence and meaning are derived from how I freely choose my actions. If I choose to behave bravely, then I am (essentially) brave. If I choose to behave in a cowardly fashion, then I am cowardly. Consequently, by acting in the world, the self gives itself meaning, but only if its actions are the result of conscious decision and choice. By deciding and choosing, I recognize my fundamental freedom, my essential nothingness. If I don't recognize this freedom that is me, I am acting in bad faith. I am pretending not to be free and I do this in order to escape the burden or anxiety of my freedom, the same anxiety I felt on the edge of the cliff.

Bad faith is something that is part of our lives. In fact, we spend most of our lives living in bad faith, a type of self-lie that makes things easier for us. Here, Sartre illustrates his point with a waiter in a Parisian café. The waiter has become all waiter. He moves as a waiter, talks as a waiter, acts as a waiter, as if he were playing a role. In doing so, he has given up his status as a free for-itself consciousness. He has given up his essential nothingness in order to become some-thing (a waiter). He is acting as a predetermined thing in-itself, as if his essence were a pre-given "waiterliness" causing him to act as a waiter. The waiter is in bad faith because he acts as if he were not free. Certainly, he gets rid of the anxiety of being a free conscious human being, but at the price of his freedom.

The example of the waiter may seem trifling. However, it depicts a way of being in the world that is very much a part of all our lives, that part where we forget we are living lives of our own making, that each instant, in Nietzschean terms, may represent the possibility for us to say "yes, I choose this moment now and forever," or not. Of course, to live in this moment of freedom would be, for both Nietzsche and Sartre, truly superhuman. Bad faith is the horizon on which our lives are sketched out, the necessary background out of which freedom may come to the fore. Living in bad faith may help us get on with our day-to-day lives, as waiters, professors, taxi drivers, sales persons etc. However, as Sartre's life in Nazi-occupied France must have shown, the biggest moral monsters may well be those who, forgetting their essential freedom (essential nothingness), are just doing their jobs, just following orders.

The problem is, however, when I attribute my meaning or essence to my actions, I thereby surrender my meaning or my essence to the views of other people. For Sartre, this is an inescapable and insoluble dilemma of existence. My actions take place in the world and in doing so, they leave me behind; they are never completely mine. I may conceive of my actions as being for-myself. However, they are always also for others and it is these others who interpret their meaning. Certainly, if I decide to behave bravely, I can be said to be brave, but this bravery of "mine" must be recognized as such by others for it to be real. In other words, I am always dependent on how other people view me, for my essence, for the truth of who I am. My meaning is held captive by others, who always determine me to be a certain way, by the way they look upon me. The secret to who I am lies in them. And yet, other people are in the same situation as me. I look upon them and hold the secret to who they are.

The struggle to regain possession of one's self, held captive by the other, is played out dialectically, in a way similar to the dialectic of recognition we witnessed in Hegel. However, where Hegel sees the struggle for freedom that takes place between selves as ending finally in mutual recognition and community, there is no such happy ending in Sartre. We are condemned to this futile struggle, to reclaim our essence from other people, as they are condemned to reclaim theirs from us. Far from creating a reassuring idea of community, the outcome of Sartre's dialectic of intersubjectivity is best expressed in his pronouncement from the play *No Exit*: Hell is other people.

In the end, Sartre encounters the same problem that Kierkegaard does, a problem that arises from the essentially individualistic nature of their existentialist philosophies. Perhaps this problem arises in any philosophy that finds ultimate truth in the life of the single individual and his or her choices and actions. In this context, it is impossible to find any substantial meaning in the broader community of individuals, whether in the form of family, society or the State. Sartre's philosophy, in *Being and Nothingness*, thus presents an important aspect of our modern individualistic condition, the difficulty we have finding real meaning through our social and political structures.

In a way, Sartre's own philosophical evolution towards more communistic forms recognizes this dilemma, without overcoming it. His attempt, in his later *Critique of Dialectical Reason*, to establish community through group revolutionary activity simply reproduces, on a more general level, the existentialist struggle between individual selves. A group of revolutionary activists may represent a particular form of community but that group, to have any meaning, must always be at odds with others. Consequently, the particular group or community simply takes on the attributes of the self-centered individual and reproduces the same problem with regard to the establishment of a meaningful world.

Our story of the self and its world has reached a point of crisis, which we might call the crisis of modern individualism. Other philosophical story-tellers might challenge the inclusion of Sartre in our story line, questioning his contemporary relevance as a protagonist. They may choose a different character and there is no shortage of present-day philosophical individualists to choose from. Few, however, express the dilemma of individualism, and our problematic relationship with the world, as starkly and honestly as Sartre. The failure of his heroic attempt to find meaning in individual existence, in a treacherous world where God is dead, is a reflection of what we perceive to be our own failure. As such, the problem of individualism is a crucial aspect of our vision of who we are today and therefore a crucial question in the concluding chapter of our story.

13. Hannah Arendt and Charles Taylor

want to end with a look at two philosophers. In the Introduction, I promised to include one woman and one live North American philosopher in order to disprove the idea that all great philosophers in the Western tradition are dead European males. One could just as easily argue, however, that the exception simply confirms the rule and that my token inclusions mean nothing. In fact, their individual particularities have nothing to do with why they appear here. Rather, it is because, as philosophical protagonists, they seem to naturally and fittingly come along at the final part of the story, the point where we realize that the story really is ours.

Specifically, both thinkers are conscious of the unhappy modern condition I described above, the difficulty in reconciling the apparently limitless demands of individual subjective freedom with meaningful social, political forms. Each seeks to renew the relationship between self and the world through an investigation of earlier forms of thought. Such a renewal implies an investigation of earlier philosophical conceptions, an investigation like the one we have been carrying out. This is why I chose them as the final thinkers in our brief story.

Hannah Arendt was born in 1906 in Hannover, Germany. She received her PhD at the prestigious University of Heidelberg, at the age of 22. She studied with German existentialists Martin Heidegger and Karl Jaspers, with whom she did her PhD. A Jew, she fled to France in 1933 to escape the Nazi regime. Then, in 1941, to escape deportation to the death camps at the hands of her collaborating French hosts, she fled to the U.S. She became an American citizen in 1951, working as an editor and for several Jewish organizations. In 1951, she also published her acclaimed *Origins of Totalitarianism*. That landmark work examines 20th-Century totalitarian regimes (Nazi Germany and Stalinist Soviet Union) as a unique form of governance, whose goal is to terrorize and isolate its citizens in order to better sweep them along, or up, in monstrous ideologies that determine every aspect of their lives. She was the first woman visiting professor at Princeton and subsequently taught at the universities of Berkeley and Chicago. In 1958, she wrote *The Human Condition*. In 1963, she wrote *Eichmann in Jerusalem*, chronicling the trial, for crimes against humanity, of Adolf Eichmann, one of the Nazi regime's top managers of the final solution. Controversially arguing against the popular, reassuring view that the Nazi regime was entirely run by monstrous moral freaks, she talks about "the banality of evil," the notion that it is rather those who are unquestioningly unexceptional who have the greatest capacity for doing bad things. After all, it was Eichmann's commonplace managerial skills and his benign disregard for the Jewish people that had allowed him to concentrate on making the death camp trains run on time. Arendt died in 1975.

Arendt is usually described as a political philosopher. Her political model is Classical Greece, the city-state of Athens, and her philosophical inspiration is Aristotle. Why? Because Aristotle described man as "a political animal," an animal whose essence it is to be political, i.e., to live in a social organization of defined political structures that is more than just a collection of individuals. For Arendt, as well, man's essence is expressed politically. However, for a post-existentialist philosopher, human essence can no longer be natural or in-born as it was with Aristotle. Man must find essence or meaning in the *way* he lives in the world. In *The Human Condition*, Arendt examines the different ways humans live in the world, and the different meanings that are derived from these ways of living.

Such a project is necessary because modern man wants nothing more than to flee the world in which he lives, either outwardly, into space, or inwardly, into himself. For the first time, humans feel they are prisoners of their meaningless world. The problem is, living in the world is the only possibility of finding meaning, through acting in the world. So, we might say that Arendt recognizes the Sartrean dilemma: the world is both that which saps us of meaning, as well as our only possibility of finding meaning, through action. The huge difference between the two thinkers is that Arendt seeks a solution to the dilemma through a specific political/social form of action. For Arendt, different ways of acting in the world imply different ways of configuring the world. Each worldly configuration reflects back on human activity, conferring meaning on it that may be impoverished or enriched. There are three levels of human activity: Labor, Work and Action.

Labor involves human activity that can be reduced to working for sustenance. It implies an activity that is carried out for purely natural reasons, like earning enough money in order to live, being a wage-slave. For Arendt, this idea of labor has become generalized with the industrial revolution. In pre-industrial France, for example, there were 143 festive holidays, not including Sundays! Now, all activities have been reduced to labor, to making a living, to earning-power. The doctor's goal is not health, but to make a living. The goal of a university education is reduced to getting a better-paid job. The world of labor has become all-pervasive. The only exception is the labor of the artist, but art is now considered to be a game, a pass-time. Thus, even the highest form of human activity has been devalued.

Hand in hand with this generalization of labor, is the consumer society. Leisure time is thought of purely as a time to consume, and both leisure and consuming become themselves a type of labor. I must get my Christmas shopping done, find the best prices, purchase leisure activities, get the most out of them, intensely. I must make them productive, recreational. Arendt contrasts this idea of leisure with the Greek ideal of *Skhole* and its attendant frugality.

In the world of Labor, the gravest danger is not leisure, but unemployment, the ultimate evil. The irony is that by using machines to produce more and more things, more and more people are forced out of work (in the 1950's, when *The Human Condition* was written, unemployment seemed to come from mechanization, not from off-shoring). In the end, we can imagine a society of consumers without work. These people will live senseless lives. There will be no notion of a higher activity to give them meaning, since their only meaning was supplied through labor. They will be no more than consumers.

The second way of acting in the world, Work, is different from Labor, in that it produces something lasting. While Labor only produces things that are meant to be consumed, the activity of Work produces things that are meant to extend beyond the life of one individual. The products of Work are inherently useful. They are tools, buildings, things fabricated by humans, which last. They may be handed down to other generations. Work is utilitarian and technological. Because it produces things that last, this activity is more meaningful than Labor, and may even confer some meaning on the baser activity of Labor. The architect can both seek to earn as much money as possible through her labor and also claim, through work, to build useful dwellings and to leave monuments behind her.

However, in our modern world, the belief that everything must be useful and managed for the greatest performance has produced a technological nightmare. The only things that have meaning are things that are useful. Human reason is reduced to technological problem solving, strategic planning, rationalizing. Through Work, the world (and the people in it) appears as something to be engineered, manipulated, calculated or maximized.

The third way of acting in the world is through Action. Action is political, in a broad sense. It consists of initiating things and speaking, or rather, speaking out. Action implies being a citizen (not just a consumer or a worker) and taking an interest and a role, however minor, in public affairs. Action implies participation beyond the merely private concerns of personal gain and utility. The model is the Athenian citizen, and the Agora, where people lay aside their private lives and become public-minded citizens, able to debate rationally on the public good.

The challenge today is that language, through science and technology, has been reduced to incomprehensible signs that serve to isolate humans. Arcane or empty technical jargon tends to make real communication impossible, and yet meaningful language is essential if humans are to have a story, continuity, and even a morality. In her book on Eichmann's trial, Arendt mentions how the manager of mass death spoke mainly in mangled clichés and borrowed expressions, making it impossible for him to articulate or enact any coherent moral positions.

Whereas the public sphere of Action should be the highest type of activity, conferring meaning on the other two spheres, today the opposite has occurred. The other two forms of activity, Labor and Work, which for the Greeks were relegated to the private sphere, have invaded the public realm of citizenship, to the point where it no longer exists. Instead of being citizens, we are consumers or trained, skilled workers. Arendt argues for a re-evaluation of the public sphere, of civic action and discourse. Such a re-evaluation would lead to reclaiming what is truly human: the human being as a political animal. A living democracy must have this level of active citizen participation and interest. Today, in concrete terms, action means taking citizenship seriously, participating in political discussion with other citizens, voting, participating in associations, getting involved in causes, even reading the newspaper!

According to Arendt, everything in modern life tends to undercut such civic participation and hence there is a real danger of totalitarianism. Since totalitarian regimes (not mere dictatorships) seek to fracture the existing social structures and to isolate citizens by breaking down the political interaction between them, these regimes can be seen to build on the tendencies of Labor and Work already at play in our world. This is perhaps the true danger in the banality of evil, the fact that we may not recognize a totalitarian form of government until it is too late, simply because everything seems so normal.

Arendt's vision, however, allows us to see that things today are not simply normal. Inspired by her knowledge of Aristotle and Classical Greece, she shows us how active political/social involvement and discourse may overcome our modern dilemma, by revealing how individual freedom is, in fact, absolutely dependent upon living, acting and speaking in a meaningful world.

Charles Taylor taught philosophy and political science at McGill University, in Montreal. Since his retirement from that institution, he has won the prestigious Templeton Prize for research on spiritual realities and acted as co-chair on a high-profile public commission into questions of multiculturalism in Quebec.

After early studies in history, at McGill, he studied philosophy and economics at Oxford, where he received his PhD in 1961. His major works are an eponymous book on Hegel, in 1975, and the magisterial *Sources of the Self*, in 1989, which is generally recognized as one of the important works of contemporary philosophy. Taylor has also written extensively on multiculturalism and the politics of recognition. Most recently, his book, *A Secular Age*, explores how our modern condition of generalized atheism arises out of the Western philosophical tradition where God is virtually omnipresent. The ideas of Taylor's that I am presenting can be found in a very approachable little book called *The Malaise of Modernity*, which was originally broadcast on CBC Radio as part of their Massey Series of Lectures, in 1991. The book summarizes the main theme from the *Sources of the Self*. In both works, Taylor describes modernity as our current way of considering ourselves and our relation to the world. This condition, which is not a happy one, is deeply involved with the notion of selfhood we have unquestioningly inherited from the past, through such philosophical articulations as the Enlightenment and Romanticism.

Taylor outlines three aspects of modern malaise or anguish. These bear a significant resemblance to Arendt's worldview and can similarly be seen as resulting from an unhappy existentialist relationship between the free self and its world.

The first malaise is individualism. This is the feeling that somehow we live in a world where the only reality is that of the individual. Existentialist philosophies, like those of Kierkegaard or Sartre, are symptomatic of the problem, as are other more contemporary, neo-liberal economic theories and practices that promote individual rights and demands over those of the community. We want to be free and yet our understanding of freedom is entirely individualistic, self-centered and lonely.

Such individualism has broken down what Taylor calls the "chain of being," the feeling of belonging to something bigger. Modern freedom no longer confines us to family, church, work or the State, so we are left to find meaning within our individual lives. We are aware that we live in a culture of narcissism, of isolation and individual pleasure-seeking and yet we have lost all hope of a broader vision. The world no longer has any meaning; it has become disenchanted. Its structures have lost their magic. As with Arendt, worldly reality has been reduced to consumable, dispensable products and pleasures. We feel the emptiness that such a world implies.

The second source of malaise stems from the dominance of what Taylor calls instrumental reason. This worldview is similar to Arendt's idea of Work. The disenchanted world is now seen from a purely utilitarian, technological, technocratic perspective. The world (and the people in it) is there as raw material, to be manipulated, calculated and processed. Economic growth, cost-benefit, efficiency and productivity are the laws that seem to rule the world. Taylor refers to both Marx and Arendt, here. Both of whom react, in their own ways, against this perceived flattening out of reality, this loss of resonance and depth.

The third modern source of worry is political; it refers to "the feared consequences for political life" that may result from our cultures of individualism and instrumental reason. Regarding instrumental reason, we see how the industrial-technological society forces us to do things that we would not otherwise do. It restricts our choices and our freedom: we make life choices entirely based on perceived usefulness, in terms of earning-power, job opportunities, future prospects, etc. We aspire to being highly trained workers, smart consumers or effective managers, high-powered sales people rather than well-rounded humans. This disturbs us.

Like Arendt, Taylor sees individualism as having potentially dangerous political repercussions. The "atomism of the self-absorbed individual," for Taylor, prevents the functioning of a "vigorous political culture," although for him the danger is one of "soft despotism" rather than totalitarianism, but then Taylor is a Canadian, not a twice-exiled German Jew. Soft despotism stems from the fact that fewer and fewer people even bother to vote, or that membership in community associations continues to decline. Thus, we lose control of the institutions that control us. We become powerless, faced with a vast bureaucratic superstructure that manages us.

However, Taylor does not merely reiterate or confirm the modern situation, the predicament we feel ourselves to be in. He proposes a solution that explicitly involves looking back to our past forms of thought, in order to rediscover the sources of modern anguish, of our run-away individualism and the technocratic world-view. He discovers that both of these cultures are actually debased forms of rich philosophical traditions that have, in his words, "rich moral backgrounds." What we experience as rampant individualism actually comes from the individual quest for authenticity, from the worthy idea of being true to oneself, of thinking independently. The sources of today's debased culture of narcissism can actually be traced back to the rich ideals of the self as free, which we saw in Descartes, Rousseau and Kant, and authentic, as we found in Kierkegaard and Sartre.

The source of "instrumental reason" also has a rich moral background, stemming from the Enlightenment desire, expressed in such thinkers as Voltaire, Diderot and Kant, to relieve the suffering of mankind through the spread of knowledge and science. The original motivation was to free humans from natural necessity, to liberate them from sickness and drudgery through reason and technology. Strikingly, however, the modern expressions of individualism and instrumental reason seem to run contrary to their original forms.

Both these original forms, freedom and enlightenment, were meant to serve humanity, not oppress it. Consequently, by rediscovering the original projects behind these forms, we are able to re-think our relation to the sources of our anguish, our individualism and our technological approach to the world. For example, rather than seeing medical technology as an end in itself, we may recall that it is there to treat and serve the whole human being or that a company's "productivity" must also include the "footprint" it leaves on humanity as a whole. Similarly, we may rediscover our own individualism as a moral quest for freedom and authenticity, and not just as empty pleasure-seeking and consumption. Personal authenticity was never meant to breed isolation. It was part of a search for a better human condition.

Arendt and Taylor indicate possible approaches to the contemporary challenge of living freely in a meaningful world. For both thinkers, we overcome our present plight by remembering past forms of thought, by recalling the history of Western philosophy. Ultimately, their lesson is this: if we forget our past forms of thought, we remain prisoners of our modern anguish.

To recognize our dilemma and attempt to overcome it, we must first make sense of it. This is what we have been doing in these pages, following the story together. Of course, the story we have followed is itself the story of making sense, of the human struggle to produce meaning. In this way, to the extent we are meaning-making beings, the story is truly our own, and only by grasping it as ours do we see that within it can be found both the source of our plight and the keys to its overcoming.